Driven by the Movement

Driven by the Movement

Reports from the Black Power Era

JoNina Abron-Ervin

Foreword by William C. Anderson

Driven by the Movement: Reports from the Black Power Era

Previous edition: *Driven by the Movement: Activists of the Black Power Era* (2011)

ISBN: 9781849356060
E-ISBN: 9781849356077
Library of Congress Control Number: 2024949076

AK Press
370 Ryan Ave. #100
Chico, CA 95973
www.akpress.org
akpress@akpress.org

AK Press
33 Tower St
Edinburgh EH6 7BN
www.akuk.com
akuk@akpress.org

The above addresses would be delighted to provide you with the latest AK Press distribution catalog, which features books, pamphlets, zines, and stylish apparel published and/or distributed by AK Press. Alternatively, visit our websites for the complete catalog, latest news, and secure ordering.

An earlier version of Chapter 3 previously appeared as "Raising the Consciousness of the People: The Black Panther Intercommunal Service, 1967–1980" in Ken Wachsberger, ed., *Insider Histories of the Vietnam Era Underground Press, Part 2* (East Lansing: Michigan State University Press, 2012).

An earlier version of Chapter 6 previously appeared as "Serving the People: The Survival Programs of the Black Panther Party" in Charles E. Jones, ed., *The Black Panther Party [Reconsidered]* (Baltimore: Black Classic Press, 1998).

Cover design by Crisis

Printed in the USA on acid-free paper

Contents

Acknowledgments

This book would not have been possible without the cooperation of the people who shared their experiences as Black Power era activists with me: Frances M. Beal; Fred Bell (a.k.a. Fahim Minkah, 1939–2018); Melvin Dickson (1940–2018); Charles (Boko) Freeman (1951–2020); Dr. Hardy Frye (1939–2021); Dr. Joyce M. Grant; Mike Hamlin (1935–2017); Joe R. Hicks (1941–2016); Gwen Johnson (a.k.a. Ayanna Ade, 1951–2013); Eva Partee McMillan (1921–2021); Fr. Earl Neil (1935–2024); Rev. C. Herbert Oliver (1925–2021); Robin (Che) Parker; Dr. Jacqueline (Jackie) Pope; Earl Rose; Tanya Russell (1938–2014); Zakiya Somburu (1951–2010); Leoduris (Lee) Rose Weisberg (1942–2011); Joye Williams; Tondalela Woolfolk (1950–1993); and Antonio (Tony) Zamora (1930–2020).

I began researching and writing this manuscript in the early 1990 s when I was an assistant (later associate) professor teaching journalism courses in the Department of English at Western Michigan University (WMU). My thanks and appreciation go to Dr. Elise Jorgens, former dean of WMU's College of Arts and Sciences, for providing me with travel funds and equipment in the early stages of my research, and to former WMU professors Dr. Gwendolyn Etter-Lewis, for encouraging me to speak about my research at academic conferences, and Dr. Shirley Clay Scott, for serving as an editor of my early grant proposals.

The following people reviewed portions of my manuscript in its early stages and gave me valuable feedback: Paul Coates, founder of Black Classic Press and former member of the Black Panther Party (BPP); Patty Hirota-Cohen, my longtime friend; three deceased Black Power era scholars: Dr. Robert L. Allen, Dr. John T. McCartney, and Dr. Ronald Walters; and my late mother, Adeline C. Erwin, who was herself an author. The Freedom Forum Journalism Professors Writing Program provided funds that I used for a quiet place to start writing this book.

Almost twenty years passed between 1992, when I began the research for this book, and 2011, when I published the first edition. I would never have considered a second edition without the encouragement of author-activist friend William C. Anderson and Lorenzo Kom'boa Ervin, my beloved comrade husband and fellow Black Power era activist. When I had given up hope that my book would ever be published, Lorenzo's unwavering belief in the importance of my manuscript kept me from total despair.

AK Press has my heartfelt thanks for believing that *Driven by the Movement* is worth a second edition. Special appreciation goes to Angelica Sgouros, my editor. Others who helped me along the way are Dale Rascoe and Wayne Curtis, both former members of the BPP. Dale created a course and hosted several virtual workshops based on interviews with some of the women featured in this book. Wayne and his wife Myrtle gave me a peaceful space away from home to put the final touches on my manuscript. Angela

Leblanc-Ernest, a longtime scholar of the BPP, digitized several interviews that were on cassette tapes.

I apologize if I have omitted the names of people who helped me with this book. I alone am responsible for any errors that may appear.

Foreword

From the Rank and File

William C. Anderson

On August 25th, 1989, a panel of three women appeared on a *Bay Sunday* broadcast after Huey P. Newton's murder, on a segment titled "Women of the Blank Panther Party." The women were Angela Davis, Ericka Huggins, and JoNina Abron, as she was then known. As they reflected on Newton's legacy and that of the Black Panther Party, and discussed topics such as the utility of the party's tactics, JoNina said something prescient: "The way the Party was and the way it was organized, it developed at a particular point in history, and it responded to a particular need . . . I think if we have something else like it in the future, it won't be exactly like that because we cannot go back to 1966. We cannot recreate that moment in history. But if the people see and feel that there is a need for something like that, similar to it, people will create it." Angela Davis agreed with JoNina, saying that we had "transcended" that moment in time. As accurate as it may be, it's often hard to overcome the nostalgia, grief, and mythology that decorate the public imagination when it comes to the revolutionary struggles that came before us. How we remember what came before has everything to do with our intentions. If we want to make critical decisions based on well-informed observations, we have to seek out as much accurate information as possible about what came before. Regarding Black history, JoNina's words in that program spoke to a more significant intervention that her work offers us.

The daughter of a minister, born in Morristown, Tennessee, and raised in Jefferson City, Missouri, she would grow up to be the last editor of one of the most radical publications the US has ever known, *The Black Panther Intercommunal News Service*. She came up through movements whose impact reshaped society, observing the civil rights movement as the child of two educators. Her mother was a music teacher, and her father, in addition to being a member of the Methodist clergy, taught philosophy and religion at Lincoln University. JoNina ultimately decided that whatever she was going to do in her future, it would be to the benefit of Black people. So, by the time she joined the Detroit chapter of the Black Panther Party, it was clear she was fulfilling a mandate that had shaped the contours of her life until that point. Her education and background primed her to play a part specific to her talents.

JoNina is a committed radical activist and thinker who has used journalism, writing, and scholarship for revolutionary purposes. Her ability to translate, edit, and shape ideas is unique and critical to activists and organizers who rely on those like her to help praxis take shape. We should ensure that people with skills like these never become an understated part of the Black radical tradition. Those who hold the pen like a sword—teachers, reporters, writers, and others—are tasked with helping masses of people understand the range of possibilities. Revolutionary work is not an easy job, and it's made harder by the fact that it may go unrewarded. There's no guarantee that people will ever know your name if you participate in a great battle, a revolutionary war, or a transformative movement. You could be lost to history despite your countless hours ensuring a victory is within reach. Such is the history of many rank-and-file activists. From the lowest soldier to a pivotal Panther, there's no guarantee you will get the honor you deserve. The ordinary people who go unseen and unheard make the world turn. Progress toward liberatory goals carries essential instruction in the minor details.

This is why JoNina Abron-Ervin's *Driven by the Movement* is a necessary text. It reflects important attention to the details because she documents the rank-and-file she herself emerged from. JoNina examines the lives of twenty-one activists of the Black Power era between 1965 and 1975. "Most of the activists interviewed for this book did not regularly appear on national television news, and for the most part, their names were not household words," she writes in her preface. "Nevertheless, they helped to bring about profound changes for Black people in their local communities."

"I am an activist and a journalist, not a historian," she tells us early on. It indeed serves her very well not to be. With history held intimately in her grasp, she doesn't feign objectivity, nor does she show preference so heavy-handed she's dogmatic. Instead, she platforms the people whose opinions and reflections she cares about to tell an important story. While we regularly read oversimplified sloganeering about "the people" and "the masses," all too often, we don't hear *from* these diverse bodies of difference. They become objectified in the cultural tendency to valorize famous leaders and grant celebrity status. This sort of instrumentalization of various "peoples" requires some undoing, and many fail to see the importance of not trivializing subtleties, omitting stories or technical minutia. It all matters.

JoNina recounts the details in the margins of the struggle for education rights, welfare rights, civil rights, and Black Power by giving voice to the regular people you likely wouldn't know about otherwise. Students taking over schools, employees breaking through racial barriers to integrate workplaces, Black Power activists confronting white supremacists, and much more fill these pages in ways that don't overemphasize the selective, self-pronounced leaders through whom history is primarily told. JoNina lets these activists tell it themselves, offering minimal narration. The result feels as if you're at a table with a chorus of speakers recounting what happened.

It isn't all glory, though; the traumas that come to the surface when recalling pasts filled with triumph and loss are present, too. Again, if we're to learn, much cannot be glossed over for a picturesque retelling that lends itself to radical folklore. A task at hand is to overcome this nostalgic relationship to the past that flourishes among radicals from younger generations. While we rightfully glorify much of what came before, we also should not do so uncritically. Not everything and everyone deserves to be treated like a blueprint. Failure is a guide to help us see what not to repeat, and if we don't know what went wrong, we may be destined to make avoidable missteps again. That's why much of what's contained in *Driven by the Movement* will feel familiar to younger generations. They'll see that we are trapped in many of the same conceits of Western radicalism and must break free from stale cycles—this text feels like a key part of the puzzle in this regard.

The book also details the expansiveness and connections

of the Black struggle nationwide. Though groups like the Black Panther Party, the Congress of Racial Equality (CORE), and the Student Nonviolent Coordinating Committee can be stripped down to popular historical caricatures, they underwent dynamic evolutions. They made changes, brokered mergers, and saw people go their separate ways. Their legacies offer insight into what an organization should and shouldn't look like in our own critical moment. What better way to realize this than hearing directly from those who experienced these shifts?

As we sit with this text, we are repeatedly reminded that JoNina's journalistic integrity is rooted in her dedication to numerous causes throughout her life. In addition to being a member of the Black Panther Party for nearly a decade and the last editor of the Black Panther newspaper, she was also once the managing editor of *Black Scholar* magazine, one of the oldest and most prestigious journals of Black studies. She's been a fierce advocate for young people and the incarcerated, as well as an active dissident resisting the police state.

While there are ongoing debates about the role of Black women in the Black Power era, JoNina was in fact situated in a predominantly woman-run and managed organization. Historian of Black women's history, Ashley D. Farmer notes:

> As the Panthers' popularity soared, so too did its female membership. Only a few years after the party's inception, women were close to half of the rank and file. Like their activist foremothers, Panther women engaged in extensive conversations over how to best conceptualize black womanhood in the party and society at large. In an effort to align their activism, political theory,

> and emancipatory goals, Panther women theorized a gender-specific version of the Panthers' political identity: the Black Revolutionary Woman. An ideal that personified gendered formulations and applications of the Panthers' political ideology, the Black Revolutionary Woman became a conduit through which female members reimagined their political and social roles.[1]

JoNina was indeed a part of a shift at a time of ideological and tactical remodeling when "in the 1970s, women emerged as formal leaders within the party. They filled multiple organizational positions, becoming directors, newspaper editors, and heads of the group's community programs. Panther women led efforts to transform the party into a locally driven, globally minded grassroots organization during its final years."[2] These facts come to life in this text through testimony. Black women had to develop their autonomy within organizations in order to make struggle also meet their needs. White feminist movements and organizations undoubtedly did not hold shared visions of liberation. "Women kept the Black Panther Party going as long as it did," JoNina once remarked when I asked her about gender oppression within the party.[3] She wasn't dismissive of the fact that, of course, problems existed,

1. Ashley D. Farmer, *Remaking Black Power: How Black Women Transformed an Era* (Chapel Hill: University of North Carolina Press, 2017), 51.
2. Ibid., 77.
3. The Institute for Social Ecology, "Black Anarchist Legacies—2023 Summer Intensive Course," panel in Detroit, May 6, 2023, YouTube, https://www.youtube.com/watch?v=Y8eWWXPu8mE (starting at 52:28).

however, she clarified that it wasn't any worse than any other left organization at the time. By emphasizing women's efforts, she takes particular pride in the fact that those who were upholding the organization's infrastructure were not doing so simply because they were subjugated but because they were the backbone and leaders from within.

This can be factored into a more recent development in her trajectory but a major one nonetheless. JoNina Abon-Ervin was eventually introduced to anarchism by her now-husband, former SNCC– and Black Panther Party–member Lorenzo Kom'boa Ervin, writer of the formative text *Anarchism and the Black Revolution*. Together, through their work as community organizers and revolutionary writers, they have shaped Black autonomy as a political tendency and organizational principle. This makes her stand out as perhaps the most visible Black woman from her generation who embraced anarchism. Though this isn't an explicitly anarchist text, her work speaks for itself and brings autonomy to life by giving voice to many, grounded by her experience as a party woman. The cohort of Black anarchists who rose from the Black Power and civil rights eras formulated their politics based on these experiences that shaped them, good and bad, to develop new people-focused perspectives that were sharply critical of earlier pitfalls.

This edition of JoNina Abron-Ervin's *Driven by the Movement* brings the original text back into print, and with new materials, this book couldn't be more timely. Amid book bans, censorship, and emboldened authoritarianism, we would do well to find inspiration in its wisdom. I have enjoyed working alongside JoNina and feel close to her work because I have learned much from her. She's an exceptional person. It's a part of my life's work to help promote materials that broaden our perspective because we *need* them. Do this book justice by reading it carefully. Ask questions about everything you can, and may we grow from the foundation that's been laid. We owe a lot to the everyday people whose names are not etched into our collective memory. JoNina helps us gather these stories and visualize other essential contexts of the movement she documents.

Here's to hoping we move closer to freedom through the details.

Preface

The course of a social revolution is never direct, never a straight line proceeding from precipitating social oppression to the desired social liberation. . . . It may culminate in complete victory, crushing defeat, or deadening stalemate. . . . The revolutionaries must contend not only with conscious reactionaries and counterrevolutionaries, but also with subtle social dynamics which act to stop or divert the revolution.

—Robert L. Allen, Black Awakening in Capitalist America: An Analytic History

The Black Power era (BPE) of 1965 to 1975 unleashed a social revolution that transformed race relations in the United States. The backbone of this revolution was ordinary African American men and women, like those profiled in this book: single working mothers, married couples, teachers, members of the clergy, autoworkers, students, welfare recipients, and others. Some put their personal lives on hold to fight battles against police brutality, the abuse of prisoners, poverty, substandard schools, gender oppression, colonialism in Africa, the Vietnam War, and other issues of the time. In the process, many BPE activists experienced "complete victory, crushing defeat, or deadening stalemate."

This book is an expanded edition of my 2011 publication *Driven by the Movement: Activists of the Black Power Era*. I was inspired to write it following the April 29, 1992, acquittal of three of the four white Los Angeles Police Department officers accused of brutally beating Black motorist Rodney King. (The fourth officer was found guilty of excessive force.) Like many other African Americans, I was stunned and outraged by the verdicts.

Watching the television coverage of the uprising that exploded in South Central Los Angeles after the acquittals, I found myself wondering what had happened to the groups of the Black Power era (BPE) that had organized against police brutality. Had Black Power era activists failed to pass on the lessons they had learned as community organizers —lessons that might have sustained public intolerance of the kind of vicious beating that Rodney King suffered?

One of the most controversial and militant groups to emerge during the Black Power era was the Black Panther Party (BPP). The Panthers' call for Black people to arm themselves in self-defense against police brutality inspired thousands of young Blacks around the country and made the group public enemy number one to US law enforcement agencies during the late 1960s. I was a member of the BPP for nearly a decade.

I first heard about the BPP near the end of my freshman year in college. In May 1967, I saw a television news report about armed Black Panthers marching into the California State Capitol building in Sacramento to protest legislation designed to disarm them. My initial reaction was that the Panthers were crazy if they thought white people were going to let them walk around with guns. Later, I would join the BPP in its mission to "serve the people, body and soul."

Thirty-seven years after the end of the BPE, the Black Lives Matter protest movement emerged in 2012 after unarmed Black teenager Trayvon Martin was shot to death by a vigilante night watchman in Sanford, Florida. After his killer, George Zimmerman, was acquitted of second-degree murder charges in May 2013, three Black female queer activists, Alicia Garza, Patrice Cullors, and Opal Tomei, created the hashtag #BlackLivesMatter.

Since Trayvon Martin's death, thousands of people chanting "Black Lives Matter" have taken to the streets in America and in solidarity marches in other countries to denounce police and white supremacist violence that led to the high-profile killings of several Black people, including: Ahmaud Arbry, Sandra Bland, Michael Brown Jr. Philando Castile, George Floyd, Eric Garner, Freddie Gray, Tyre Nichols, Tamir Rice, Walter Scott, Breonna Taylor, and many others. Viral cell phone footage spread around the world of Floyd, a forty-six-year-old Black man, as he was choked to death by a white police officer in Minneapolis, Minnesota in May 2020.

By 1991, when Los Angeles police officers savagely beat Rodney King, racial profiling and paramilitary policing had already been in use by US police agencies since 1980. Since then, police terror in America has only become deadlier. A 2019 report by the *Lancet*, the prestigious British medical-legal journal, revealed that over 35,000 people had been killed by American police since 1980. Police killed at least 1,232 people in 2023, according to the research group Mapping Police Violence, the deadliest year since it had started its recordkeeping, and over 1,000 people every year for decades.

In 1967, the FBI launched a "black nationalist hate" counterintelligence program (known as COINTELPRO) to "expose, disrupt, misdirect, discredit or otherwise neutralize" the Black liberation struggle in America. As a result, numerous BPE activists suffered brutal and murderous repression. They were killed, their organizations were destroyed, and many were imprisoned for decades. Despite this suppression, the social revolution ignited during the Black Power era caused a temporary halt to the efforts of politicians, white supremacists, and big business who sought to establish an authoritarian government in America.

The Black Panther Party organized to fight fascism in America. After organizing the 1969 United Front Against Fascism conference, the BPP created the National Committee to Combat Fascism (NCCF). The NCCF helped to stop then–President Richard Nixon's attempt to create a presidential dictatorship and helped to slow the spread of fascism at that time. Unlike their predecessors of the BPE, contemporary Black activists must do their work during a dangerous time when America faces the possibility of a fascist dictatorship. This threat has been bolstered by the Republican Party's support of Project 2025 and by a June 2024 decision by the US Supreme Court granting the president of the United States immunity from all criminal acts while in office. This ruling creates a presidential dictatorship.

Project 2025, "The Presidential Transition Project," is an over 900-page manifesto created by the conservative Heritage Foundation proposing that the president of the United States take total control of the government, making Congress and the courts subservient branches of government. At this writing, the 2024 presidential election is a few months away. However, if Republican Party presidential candidate Donald Trump defeats US vice president Kamala Harris, the Democratic Party nominee following Joe Biden's withdrawal from seeking a second term, Project 2025 could be put in place almost immediately unless anti-authoritarian activists organize and join forces to defeat it.

Many of the nationally recognized figures of the BPE have written books and articles. However, as historian Rhonda Y. Williams has pointed out, "Black Power politics . . . did not just merely happen at the national or international level . . . but also occurred in local communities where Black people, who were just fed up, responded to unsympathetic and oppressive state policies." This book surveys the work and experiences of twenty-one African American activists during the Black Power era. Most of the activists interviewed for this book did not make national news headlines, and for the most part, their names were not household words. Nevertheless, they helped to bring about profound changes for Black people in their local communities and nationwide, in some cases. The beliefs and activities of BPE activists and groups varied from region to region. The activists interviewed for this book worked in California, Illinois, Indiana, Massachusetts, Michigan, Mississippi, New Jersey, New York, Tennessee, and Texas. The late sociologist Robert L. Allen, who wrote one of the first major books about the BPE, criticized the "myopic view" of scholars and journalists who maintain that the era was "little more than . . . a bizarre deviation from the mainstream civil rights movement."

The interviews for my book were conducted between 1992 and 1997, roughly twenty years since the end of the BPE in 1975. The majority of the activists then ranged in age from the midforties to the late sixties. Two were in their seventies. Some activists adopted traditional African names after the BPE ended. Those names will be noted. However, as BPE activists, they were primarily known by their birth names, which will be used throughout the book. For clarity and grammar, I have edited the activists' remarks where necessary, paying careful attention to retaining the essence of their comments. However, as literary critic Jewel Parker Rhodes has said: "Memoirs are less about the chronology of events and more about the spiritual and emotional quality of life. . . . Memories are like a scrapbook of polaroids in our minds." Given the long passage of time between the end of the BPE and the interviews, I focused on the activists' recollections and conclusions about their experiences. Where necessary, I provide background information to help put certain events into context for readers who may not be familiar with them.

Sociologist Sarah Lawrence-Lightfoot points out, "journeyers and their navigators [who tell] life stories . . . both know that the stories they tell will not be a factual representation of history or experience. Our search is not for a rendering of objective truth or replicable evidence, but for the reconstruction and reinterpretation of experience." Historian Peniel E. Joseph maintains that a more holistic approach is needed for the study of BPE activism: "Too often, historical accounts . . . are crafted as 'cold histories' that like the *Dragnet* television series, ask for 'just the facts' . . . such narratives need to include discussion of the psychological, emotional, and physical effects of Black Power activism." For a variety of reasons, many BPE activists in the United States disagree about what we accomplished, what we didn't, and why.

This book is not a historical, political, or sociological study of the Black Power era. Nor is it an oral history. I am not an historian. For more than fifty years, I have been a community organizer and a journalist. Historian Kenneth J. Heineman argues that social activists of the 1960s have "exaggerated their own historical importance, creating in the process numerous myths concerning the causes with which they identified." Therefore, he maintains, historians who are sympathetic to the causes of social activists whom they interview should "maintain some emotional and intellectual distance" from their subjects. Journalists, too, are expected to provide objective reports of the people and events they write about. However, it is impossible for me to be dispassionate when writing about the BPE, in which I was a participant for part of my young adult life. Indeed, my personal experiences during this turbulent period in American history have allowed me to contribute background information that may be useful to readers. Using my training as a journalist, I have attempted to provide some snapshots of the lives and work of several BPE activists. In a sense, this book is their collective memoir.

The book is organized as follows: chapter 1 offers an overview of some of the key events, people, and organizations of the early years of the BPE. In chapter 2, the activists recall what motivated them to get involved in the Black liberation struggle. Chapter 3 provides a history of the Black Panther Party's newspaper, which averaged weekly sales of about 100,000 between 1968 and 1971. In chapter 4, the activists describe the work they did. In chapter 5, they recall some of the problems they encountered and the personal sacrifices they made while doing their work. Chapter 6 describes the BPP's community service programs. Chapter

7 recounts the experiences of five members of the Black Panther Party—which FBI director J. Edgar Hoover called "the greatest threat to the internal security of the country." Finally, in the Epilogue, some of the activists provide their personal assessments of the BPE and reflect on what they learned and what lessons the BPE may have for Black activists engaged in contemporary community organizing.

Here, I will clarify my use of three terms: Black Power era, Black, and African American. The Black Power movement is the common term used by scholars to describe Black-nationalist activity in the United States between 1965 and 1975. However, there were numerous African American groups that sprang up during the BPE, most of which were not unified into a single movement. In addition, some of the people whom I interviewed were simultaneously activists in Black and in multiracial organizations. Therefore, except when directly quoting the activists, I will use the term "Black Power era" instead of "Black Power movement." Black and African American will be used interchangeably.

I hope that contemporary Black activists will gain insights and learn lessons from this book that will help them to fight the current threat of America becoming a fascist state and to continue the ongoing Black liberation struggle, never forgetting that "the course of a social revolution is never direct, never a straight line."

Driven by the Movement

CHAPTER 1

"They Don't Want to Hear That Turn-the-Other Cheek Stuff"

"Now you're facing a situation where the young Negro's coming up. They don't want to hear that 'turn-the-other cheek stuff,' no. . . . There's a new deal coming in." This comment by Malcolm X in 1964 was perhaps an apt description of the new mood then beginning to develop in much of Black America. An in-depth discussion of Malcolm's role and influence on Black consciousness in the United States from 1965 to 1975 is beyond the scope of this book. Suffice it to say here that scholars have described Malcolm as the "fearless propagandist" of the Black Power era, the "spiritual adviser in absentia for a generation" of Black activists; and "a transitional figure in the continuum of Afro-American activism." His assassination in February 1965 helped to launch the Black Power era and initiated a new start, "a benchmark in the historical progression of Black protest thought."

Less than a month after Malcolm's murder, an integrated group of peaceful voting rights marchers were brutally beaten by police outside Selma, Alabama. The infamous attack on the Edmund Pettus Bridge on March 7, 1965, which was broadcast on national television, contributed to the growing dissent of many Blacks toward peaceful integration. In rural Lowndes County, near Selma, Black farmers had long believed in self-defense and owned guns, which they did not hesitate to use when they believed it was necessary. Soon after the Selma march, the Lowndes County Freedom Organization (LCFO), an all-Black independent political party, was formed. Its symbol was a snarling black panther, described by LCFO chairman John Hulett as "an animal that when . . . pressured . . . moves back until it is cornered, and then it comes out fighting for life or death." According to Hulett, "We felt we had been pushed back long enough and that it was time for Negroes to come out and take over."

Some five months after the Selma protest, the predominantly Black Los Angeles community of Watts erupted in racial violence following the arrest and beating of a Black man for a traffic violation. When the five-day rebellion in August 1965 ended, it had claimed the lives of at least thirty-four people (most of whom were Black), over nine hundred injuries, over four thousand arrests, and some $200 million in property damages. According to the commission appointed by then–California governor Edmund G. Brown Sr. to investigate the causes of the Watts uprising: "The existing breach [between Blacks and whites] if allowed to persist, could in time split our society irretrievably."

The founding of the LCFO and the Watts rebellion were two significant events of 1965 that signaled a new mood in Black America. There would be other signs in 1966. In May that year, Congressman Adam Clayton Powell Jr. addressed the graduating class at Howard University. Powell, then chairman of the House Education and Labor Committee and one of the most powerful Black political leaders in America, told the Howard graduates: "Human rights are

God-given. Civil rights are man-made. . . . Our life must be purposed to implement human rights. . . . To demand these God-given rights is to seek Black Power—the power to build black institutions of splendid achievement."

On June 16, 1966, some three weeks after Powell's speech, a few hundred civil rights activists gathered for a rally in Greenwood, Mississippi, in preparation for a march to protest the shooting ten days earlier of James Meredith, the first African American to graduate from the University of Mississippi. Meredith was shot a day after he began his one-man "March Against Fear" through his home state. The last speaker at the rally was Stokely Carmichael (Kwame Ture), chairman of the Student Nonviolent Coordinating Committee (SNCC). SNCC members had worked tirelessly since 1960 to end the political disenfranchisement of Blacks in Mississippi and elsewhere in the South. Despite their efforts, Black people in the bastion of the old Confederacy not only remained largely voteless but were also among the poorest people in America. Like many veteran SNCC activists, Carmichael had concluded that nonviolent marches and demonstrations would not significantly change the racial oppression of Mississippi Blacks or of poor Blacks in the urban North. New methods and strategies were needed.

SNCC organizer Willie (Mukasa) Ricks provided one such strategy. He coined the slogan "Black Power for Black people" that SNCC workers had used in Alabama. At the Greenwood rally, Carmichael ignited the audience by repeating a shortened version of the slogan, "Black Power." Thus was launched the new mantra of the Black liberation struggle in America. The slogan immediately proved controversial, drawing condemnation from white establishment news media and various interpretations by Blacks.

Another key event in the unfolding of the Black Power era occurred in September 1966, when Congressman Powell convened a Black Power Planning Conference (BPPC) in Washington, DC, attended by some one hundred Black leaders and activists. Dr. Nathan Wright, executive director of the department of urban work of the Episcopal diocese in Newark, New Jersey, was appointed chairman of the conference's planning committee. Although SNCC had provided the slogan that helped to launch the new era of Black consciousness, the organization did not send a representative to the BPPC. SNCC leaders believed that Powell and other established Black leaders were attempting to co-opt the new momentum in the Black struggle.

Meanwhile, in Oakland, California, two Black college students, Huey P. Newton and Bobby Seale, founded the Black Panther Party for Self-Defense on October 15, 1966.

Initially known for its armed "community patrols" that monitored police misconduct and later for serving free hot breakfasts to kids before they went to school, the BPP was "arguably the premier Black left organization of the African American liberation struggle." (See chapter 5 for coverage of the BPP.)

In an effort to destroy the growing Black liberation movement, the FBI unleashed its counterintelligence program (COINTELPRO) in August 1967, "to expose, disrupt, misdirect, or otherwise neutralize the activities of black-nationalist hate-type organizations and their leadership." COINTELPRO's initial targets included SNCC and two of its leaders, H. "Rap" Brown (Jamil Abdullah Al-Amin) and Stokely Carmichael (Kwame Ture); Dr. Martin Luther King Jr. and the Southern Christian Leadership Conference (SCLC), a civil rights group in which King served as the first president; the Nation of Islam and its leader, Elijah Muhammad; and the Revolutionary Action Movement (RAM) and its leader, Max Stanford (Akbar Muhammad Ahmad). The US Senate Intelligence Committee later characterized COINTELPRO's techniques as "deplorable . . . [and] intolerable in a democratic society."

COINTELPRO was, in part, the FBI's response to the fact that many Blacks, particularly youth, were increasingly rejecting the "turn-the-other-cheek" philosophy that prevailed in the civil rights movement. Between 1964 and 1967, Black rebellions rocked such northern cities as Philadelphia, Rochester (New York), Chicago, Omaha, Cleveland, Detroit, and Newark, New Jersey. According to the Report of the National Advisory Commission on Civil Disorders (known as the Kerner Commission), which investigated the causes of the civil disorders in the summer of 1967, a "deep hostility" between poor Black communities and the police was a primary cause of these uprisings. The commission warned that America was "moving toward two societies, one black, one white—separate and unequal."

Newark, scene of one of the nation's bloodiest racial disorders in the late 1960s, was the site of the first national Black Power Conference. Held in July 1967, the conference began just three days after the end of the city's Black rebellion. Delegates from twenty-six states, 286 Black or predominantly Black organizations of various political persuasions, and two foreign countries came to this gathering "for black people to talk to black people on what black people must do to empower black communities." The Black Power Manifesto adopted by conference delegates declared: "Black people have consistently expended a large part of our energy and resources reacting to white definition. It is imperative that we begin to develop the organizational and technical competence to initiate and enact our own programs." Resolutions from the conference workshops urged Blacks to create neighborhood credit unions in Black communities, elect more Black members to Congress, and establish community control of schools in Black neighborhoods. One of the few major civil rights leaders to attend the conference was Floyd McKissick, national director of the Congress of Racial Equality (CORE), which had adopted the ideology of Black Power at its 1966 convention. Others who did not attend the conference included Martin Luther King Jr., Roy Wilkins (national secretary of the NAACP), Whitney Young (chairman of the National Urban League), and Congressman Powell. The congressman was scheduled to address the delegates but did not attend the conference due to efforts then underway to unseat him as the chairman of a powerful congressional committee. Regarding the major civil rights leaders who did not attend the Black Power Conference: "Nobody missed them," said one Black journalist.

These events were some of the key public indicators that the Black Power era had arrived. During the decade of 1965–1975, many Blacks across the country would reexamine their previous assumptions about how best to wage the Black struggle for racial, social, and political equality in the United States. It is not the intent of this book to examine the different ideologies of Black Power. Despite their differences, however, Black Power era activists generally advocated "community control" of the economic and political institutions in Black America.

The late Black playwright August Wilson said, "The Black Power Movement . . . was the kiln in which I was fired." Who were some of the "young Negroes coming up" and their elders who were "fired up" by Black Power? What inspired some of them to place their new consciousness in service to the Black liberation struggle in America?

CHAPTER 2

Black and Proud

When James Brown came out with that song, "Say It Loud, I'm Black and I'm Proud," I used to holler [it] out the car. I was really stupid about it. It was like my spirit was being renewed.

—Tanya Russell, Black Power era activist

To Hardy Frye, hollering out his Black pride seemed unnecessary in Tuskegee, Alabama, where he was born in 1939. The east central Alabama city is the location of Tuskegee University (formerly Tuskegee Institute), one of the oldest African American colleges in the United States. When Hardy was growing up in the 1940s and 1950s, Black colleges played a pivotal role in segregated southern Black communities like Tuskegee.

"Everything I did as a kid, I did on the campus [of Tuskegee Institute]," Hardy said. "Everything [in the town] was segregated. My father had to drive forty miles to buy groceries. It wasn't just segregated; they had nothing for Blacks. . . . White people were there. We knew who they were. But they were irrelevant to my growing up. When I say that, people look at me like I'm crazy. They can't imagine someone growing up in the South where white people are irrelevant."

In 1956 Hardy dropped out of high school to join the US Army, where he said he encountered racism "in a meaningful fashion" for the first time in his life. After he left the army in 1959, he moved to Los Angeles where he lived for a while with his sister in the Black community of Watts. Life for Hardy in the urban Black world of Los Angeles was much different from his life in the rural Black world outside Tuskegee. While looking for work, he was confronted with racism. "Every day I would put on a clean shirt and a suit and check on jobs. I couldn't find a job. I was beginning to understand something about racism outside of the military," he said. Newly married and often without steady employment, Hardy sometimes made gambling collections for a Black woman who supplemented her income as a health care worker. "Without a doubt, I'd bring her every penny. I had this tremendous admiration for her. She was a strong, working-class Black woman, like my parents," Hardy said.

Hardy received his baptism in political activism in the summer of 1960 when the Democratic National Convention was held in Los Angeles. Some demonstrators at the convention wanted presidential nominee John F. Kennedy to make a statement on civil rights, and to put pressure on him they organized a picket line outside the Los Angeles Coliseum where the convention was held. Hardy was recruited to join the picket line, which included several members of CORE, then a leading civil rights organization. Hardy subsequently joined the CORE chapter in Los Angeles. On a national level, CORE would later embrace Black Power.

As described in chapter 1, Watts, Los Angeles, erupted in

August 1965 after the arrest of a Black man who allegedly resisted arrest during a traffic stop by a white police officer. At least thirty-four people, most of whom were Black, died during the five-day rebellion. Joe Hicks, a Watts native, lived near one of the flash points of the rebellion. Then a twenty-four-year-old husband and father, Joe worked at a local gas company. While growing up, he said, he listened to his father, a "peripheral Garveyite," talk about Black politics. After the Watts rebellion, Joe said: "I got in some real serious arguments with white folks at my job. They would say. . . . 'Why are you guys [Blacks] burning down your community?' Middle-class Black folks were in many ways copying similar kinds of class attitudes, in relation to poor Black folks who were responding to oppression." Jarred out of his complacency after the Watts rebellion, Joe started to attend meetings of the Black Congress.

A coalition of organizations, the Black Congress was then one of the largest Black activist groups in Los Angeles. Members would "argue out various positions and strategies," Joe said. One of the groups in the congress was an organization called US (meaning "us" Blacks as opposed to "them" whites). US emphasized culture as the catalyst for organizing the Black community, a viewpoint that Joe shared. "I was very much a believer at that time that one of the things that Black folks were missing was a sense of identity about a whole history linking them to [Africa], that gave [American] Blacks a new identity, purpose and direction," he said. Impressed with the leadership of the US chairman, Maulana (Ron) Karenga, who was a well-known proponent of Black cultural nationalism, Joe said he decided to join the US organization. Living a "dual existence" as a Black activist and the breadwinner for his wife and child ("I understood that I had to keep a j-o-b"), Joe worked in the US organization in the evenings and on weekends. He used his skills in communications to help produce the group's publications.

A common belief among many advocates of Black Power was their desire for community control of the economic, political, and social institutions in Black America. The Ocean Hill–Brownsville (OHB) movement in Brooklyn, New York, which began in 1966, was one of the first organized efforts to advocate community control of the schools. Rev. C. Herbert Oliver, a Presbyterian minister, was a leader of the movement. Born in 1925 in Birmingham, Alabama, into a family of nine children, Reverend Oliver earned his bachelor's degree in 1947. Following the murder of a Black voter registration activist by white racists in Alabama, he decided to join the civil rights movement. "I was standing looking at [the man's body] and thinking that if something wasn't done about racism, one day I'd be laying here," he later recalled. "I said that I'm going to do something about it if ever the opportunity comes."

Reverend Oliver was arrested and jailed in Birmingham in 1948 for allowing a civil rights group to hold a voter registration seminar at his church. He was later cleared of all charges but was forced to leave town with his wife and infant child because the ensuing publicity prevented him from keeping a job. Following the death of his father in 1959, Reverend Oliver returned to Birmingham, where he spent the next six years as the executive secretary of a group that documented information about alleged civil rights violations in the Birmingham area. "We documented about 100 such cases in a five-year period and circulated the information to hundreds of congressmen, law enforcement agencies, and interested people in order to focus on the abuses of the Birmingham Police Department," Oliver said. "I think that had a very positive effect of cutting down on the police brutality in the area because by 1965 when I left there, we only had about a dozen cases to document whereas in one year we had had over 100."

Reverend Oliver became the pastor of Westminster Presbyterian Church in Brooklyn, New York, in 1965. Like many parents in Brooklyn, he was critical of the quality of education his children received in the public schools. In Birmingham, one of his sons had been an honors student in math. After one year in Brooklyn public schools, his son was flunking math. When Oliver went to talk to his son's math teacher about the boy's grades, the teacher told him that his son was doing fine. "My son was flunking math," Oliver said, "but this teacher told me my son was doing fine! I was angry. I can still feel the anger." Concerned parents organized the Ocean Hill–Brownsville movement to overhaul Brooklyn's deteriorating public school system. When the OHB local school board was created, some members of Reverend Oliver's church urged him to get on the board. He did and was subsequently elected chairman.

There was also a movement in the late 1960s for community-controlled schools in Boston. Joyce Grant, a public-school teacher, was an activist in that movement. She was born in Boston in 1938, the only child of West Indian immigrants. Her father was a welder who worked on nuclear submarines, and her mother was a banker. "I can remember as a small child having a bank account. My mother insisted that I have a bank account and know how to use money," Joyce said. When she was fourteen, her mother died, which made Joyce's teenage years difficult. (Her father later remarried.) Joyce was active in the Episcopalian

Church and was president of the student government and her junior and senior classes in high school. Racism prevented Joyce from getting a teaching job in Boston after she graduated from the State Teachers College at Boston. Following a brief teaching stint in Cincinnati, she returned to Boston and was finally able to get a teaching job. She stopped teaching in the early 1960s to become the full-time secretary of the Massachusetts Freedom Movement (MFM), a multiracial coalition of civil rights and community organizations. "The director of MFM said he needed somebody to be his Girl Friday, his secretary. I don't know what possessed me to say I'd do it. I already had ten things cooking, [but] I quit teaching school the next day [and went to work for the MFM]," Joyce said.

The MFM was active in the fight to end segregation in Boston's public schools. "You would have thought that [Boston] School Committee members were in Mississippi. That's how blatantly racist they were and didn't make any bones about it. Parents were simply fed up. They were fed up with not having heat in schools, schools that didn't have materials, kids [who had hundreds] of substitutes a year. Things weren't right," Joyce said. "It was a wonderful time because it was a time when the national tenor was in support of [civil rights]. People felt they could take the risks. I remember feeling like if you got arrested, twenty-five hundred people would come out and save you. If you got arrested in Boston today, you'd be in serious trouble. One of the wonders of the movement was that people of different classes and races really came together to work. We worked around the clock. This was not eight to five. This was high negotiations with organizations and businesses to make our point clear."

By 1965, Jacqueline (Jackie) Pope had returned to Brooklyn, her childhood home. Born in the early 1940s in Philadelphia, she grew up in Brooklyn in a middle-class Black family, the daughter of a nurse and an electronics technician. After returning to Philadelphia to complete high school, Jackie earned a degree as an X-ray technician and got married. When she was pregnant with her fourth daughter, she and her husband separated. Back in Brooklyn in 1965, Jackie struggled to raise her four young daughters alone. Unable to find a job, she became a welfare recipient. At the time, the Catholic Church in Brooklyn was very active in the growing welfare rights movement and provided significant funding for the movement. A nun at Our Lady of Victory Catholic School, which Jackie's oldest daughter attended, took Jackie under her wing.

"Sister Mary saw me one day walking down the street almost in tears because I knew school was about to open, and I had no money to buy any school clothes for my kids or to get them in any decent school," Jackie said. "Sister Mary stopped me, and we struck up a friendship. She gave me vouchers to get school clothes, a school uniform for my oldest daughter and a scholarship grant. All my daughters went to the school. Sister Mary and I got close. As a result, I converted to Catholicism."

When Sister Mary invited Jackie to attend an educational meeting about the welfare system, Jackie resisted at first. "I didn't want to be hobnobbing with people on public assistance because I was on public assistance," she said. "I didn't want people to know that. [I thought] I was better than public assistance recipients." However, she attended the meeting, from which eventually grew the largest chapter of the National Welfare Rights Organization (NWRO) in the

United States. Jackie would become a local and a national NWRO leader.

In some Black Power era organizations, the role of women in the Black struggle was a controversial issue. An interracial group of women in SNCC organized a discussion on this topic. One of those women was Frances M. Beal. To Frances, male chauvinism was yet another form of oppression in her life, along with the racial and religious bigotry she experienced as the daughter of a Jewish mother and an African American father. Frances was born in 1940 in the small upstate New York community of Binghamton. "Binghamton was considered 'up South' by many people because it had some of the same repressive characteristics that you had in the South, but this was the North," Frances said. "It was very difficult to live in an extremely racist situation. My mother was very important in trying to make us proud about our racial background." Frances's father was a civil engineer. Because of racism, he could not get a job in his field and had to work as a truck driver to support his family.

Frances attended the University of Wisconsin and in the early 1960s was an exchange student at the University of Paris. There she met several students from African countries that had recently won their independence from European colonialism. "People would hang out in the cafés and talk about liberation and freedom in a way that had not yet happened in the United States. The ideas of talking about the mechanisms of power and powerlessness, whether it was from being in a colonial situation or because you were Black in America, were very popular. I was very impressed by those kinds of thoughts and ideas," Frances said. In Paris, she also met several African American expatriates, including musicians and writers, among them novelist Richard Wright, who had settled in Paris to escape the racism of America. There was racial discrimination in Paris, but the Black expatriates, Frances explained, "could live a little more dignified type of life. Even to be able to go someplace and live in a nonsegregated society was a big step forward for a number of the musicians." Frances would return to the United States during the summers, which kept her up to date on what was happening in the civil rights movement—the subject of some articles she wrote for the French press.

Frances married her high school sweetheart and gave birth to two daughters during the six years she lived in France. She returned to America to work in Alabama in the historic SNCC southern voter registration drive in the 1964 Freedom Summer project. In 1966, following the breakup of her marriage, Frances and her two young daughters moved to New York City, where Frances worked with the campaign of SNCC's International Affairs Commission against the war in Vietnam. When the debate over the "woman question" erupted in SNCC, Frances would play a major role.

SNCC was not the only Black Power era organization in which male chauvinism was an issue. In Kalamazoo, Michigan, Joye Williams encountered the problem in one of the city's Black Power organizations. Joye grew up in the early 1950s in a segregated Black community in Pine Bluff, Arkansas. After attending a local college for two years, she came to Kalamazoo in 1966 to study occupational therapy at Western Michigan University. Black students at the university organized the Black Action Movement (BAM), and after the assassination of Martin Luther King Jr. on April 4, 1968, BAM members took over Western's student union. "I was in class that day and was not aware that BAM had taken over the union," Joye recalled. "I knew the leaders of BAM. They told me that I should not be in class. I joined the group. That was my first exposure to Black protest."

Joye subsequently earned a bachelor's degree and got married. In 1969 her husband joined the Kalamazoo branch of the Black Topographical Research Center ("the Top"), a Black Power era group that supported the creation of an independent Black nation comprising Alabama, Georgia, Louisiana, Mississippi, and South Carolina. "[My husband] was very frustrated with the white power structure. He quit a couple of good jobs because of his frustration. He ran into some men who had organized the Top. . . . He was very enchanted with it." As Joye would find out, women were excluded from leadership and decision-making roles at the Top.

Many Black female activists during the time found it difficult to identify with some of the actions of radical white feminists. According to Leoduris (Lee) Rose (now Lee Weisberg), who was a Black Power era activist in California, "It was hard to be a feminist when I was a mother of three," she would later recall. "At the time, I found that a contradiction. When the feminist movement first came out in California, it completely rejected everything that had to do with being a woman. I used to shave my legs. Feminists didn't. They were burning bras. When you have to get attention, you do the radical things to get attention. I did not want to do those kinds of things."

Lee was born in Galveston, Texas, in 1942. As a child, she moved with her mother and stepfather to San Francisco, where she spent most of her childhood and attended school. In the early 1960s, Lee married Earl Rose and subsequently gave birth to three sons. By 1970, she and Earl, a marine, and their sons lived at Camp Pendleton, the Marine Corps base in Southern California. National opposition to the Vietnam War had become widespread. "There were all these demonstrations in the street," Lee said. "Something was happening every day. The Black servicemen were giving the Black Power salute. They'd talk about their brothers being killed in Vietnam and being mistreated in the military. It was exciting to be involved in something like that and to care about it. Everybody cared about each other."

Lee's initial political involvement was with the United Farm Workers, which was conducting a national boycott against table grapes. Her husband knew a boycott organizer and urged Lee to attend one of the meetings. "It was a catalyst, going to that one meeting and seeing that there were people who were caring, who cared as I did," Lee said. Subsequently, she joined the boycott picket lines at Safeway stores where the grapes were sold. After Earl was discharged from the Marine Corps, the family moved to San Francisco. There Lee became active in several Black and multiracial organizations. She helped to serve food in the BPP's free breakfast program for children, and she and Earl later joined the Black Workers Congress, a Marxist-Leninist organization founded by Black autoworkers and community activists in Detroit.

For Earl Rose, the war in Vietnam was the catalyst for his political activism. The oldest child and only son in a large Black family, Earl was born in 1939 in San Francisco and grew up across the Bay Bridge in Oakland. After attending San Francisco City College, he joined the Marine Corps in 1960. He said: "I wanted to become a war hero. I was real young, ready to go, ready to make my mark, another John Wayne, I guess. I wanted to be that type of person, you know, high-profile. I was inspired by John F. Kennedy's statement, 'Ask not what your country can do for you—ask what you can do for your country.' I was disillusioned with racism. The military was my way out of the ghetto and my way of changing my life."

When Earl joined the marines, the Kennedy administration was gradually escalating US support for South Vietnam in its war with communist North Vietnam. Based in Okinawa during his first tour of duty, Earl said he was a member of a team ready for any type of incident. "It was sort of hooked up with the Southeast Asia Treaty Organization and that whole combined force. We were the shock troops. If anything happened, we were there." By the end of 1965, President Lyndon Johnson had begun a major escalation of US military forces in Southeast Asia. Consequently, antiwar sentiments grew in Black America. Earl began his second tour of duty in the summer of 1965 and was based in South Vietnam. It was there that his political consciousness began to develop. "We went over there to stop the [communist] aggression. That's what we were told, but we found out there was no aggression," Earl said. "When we went on patrols and stuff, we would see signs that [the Vietnamese] people were not our enemies and that we should be home fighting for our own rights. I was in a situation where I was in the battalion headquarters. I was close to a lot of military officers. The war in Vietnam was not about [North Vietnamese] aggression. It was about oil. I saw Shell Oil and a lot of American companies over there benefiting from the war. I was in a battalion [where] we were plotting land where hotels could easily be built, that kind of thing."

His experiences as a Black soldier in Vietnam led Earl to eventually oppose the war. He said, "When you leave the United States, you see what the US really is. You see it objectively. You become an American when you leave the United States. You're not just Black. You identify yourself as a Black American, but people only see you as an American, and that means a whole different thing." When he returned to Camp Pendleton in California in 1970, Earl passed out leaflets "to raise the consciousness of the GIs that this war was not for us." Many Black marines agreed with him, he said. Black Power had entered the US military.

Another Black ex-GI, Mike Hamlin, began his activism in Detroit in the early 1960s. Born in Mississippi in 1935, Mike moved to Detroit with his family when he was twelve. After finishing high school, he attended the University of Michigan for two-and-a-half years before he ran out of money and joined the army. After his discharge in 1960 at age twenty-five, he returned to Detroit "an angry Black man," Mike said. "I had discovered the lie that was America, the hypocrisy . . . the falsehoods that we had all been brought up under. From 1960 on, I looked for ways in which to struggle."

Mike became acquainted with several Black-nationalist activists in Detroit. Eventually he became part of a core of young Black activists who "listened religiously" to Malcolm X and "voraciously consumed" the writings of such internationally known revolutionary leaders and thinkers as Frantz Fanon, Che Guevara, Kwame Nkrumah, Julius Nyerere, and Sékou Touré. Mike and his comrades organized against police brutality, advocated armed struggle, and "were very serious about trying to put a stop to the outrageous conditions [Black] people lived under," he said. The activists also raised money to support the work of civil rights organizations in the South. While pursuing his political activism,

Mike worked as a circulation truck driver and newspaper carrier manager for the *Detroit News*.

By 1966, when Stokely Carmichael began to popularize the Black Power slogan, the network of Black activists to which Mike belonged had concluded that Marxism was the best tool for the Black struggle in America. He explained: "We had encountered various leftist . . . groups. None of them had any faith in the working class. We had developed an analysis . . . that the Black worker was different than the white worker, that the Black worker had revolutionary potential and that we could build Black workers with a revolutionary, Marxist program. Not only would that advance the cause of Blacks and workers generally, but it would demonstrate to these folks who had lost faith that the working class still had revolutionary potential."

Mike and his Black Marxist comrades decided that their organizing tool would be a newspaper, which they hoped would attract people who had revolutionary ideas like theirs. At the *Detroit News*, Mike met John Watson, a part-time student at Wayne State University. "John was a genius. He had the capability of learning any kind of technical equipment as well as the intellectual capacity," Mike said. Together the two launched a newspaper, the *Inner City Voice*. Mike borrowed money to start the newspaper, which began publication in September 1967, some two months after a large Black rebellion shook Detroit.

In 1965 Congress enacted affirmative action guidelines that required predominantly white colleges and universities that received federal funds to step up their recruitment of African American students, faculty, and staff. Inspired by Black Power ideologies and politics, Black students at predominantly white colleges and universities demanded courses and activities that reflected the Black experience. When officials at some universities were slow to meet these demands, some Black students organized protests to get what they wanted. One such protest occurred at the University of Illinois in Champaign-Urbana, where in 1968 the university created a program to recruit Black students. As a result, some five hundred Black students were enrolled at the university. "When those five hundred students arrived at the campus, they thought they had a massive number," said Antonio (Tony) Zamora, who was then a local community activist and a professional musician. "But when the [full student body of] twenty-seven thousand or twenty-eight thousand arrived, it sort of inundated the Black students in what they were up against. They encountered all kinds of overt and covert racism, and, as a result of that, they rebelled and took over the student union." Over two hundred Black students were arrested as a result, Tony said.

Among their demands were a Black studies program, more Black faculty, and a Black cultural center.

"The university responded," Tony explained. "It formed an Afro-American Commission, which was the umbrella for three phases of programming that would go on at the university: a Black studies department, Afro-American cultural programs, and a community base, which would serve as an outreach to the community to provide an entrée to meet some of the needs of the African American community." In 1969 the Afro-American Cultural Center opened on campus.

When the center's first director left the job, Tony was asked to take over. Born in the late 1930s, Tony had helped picket stores and businesses in the Champaign-Urbana area that discriminated against Blacks during the late 1950s and early 1960s. He was the leader of a jazz band, and he and his band members frequently performed in New York City, where they were in contact with Black poets, novelists, playwrights, and musicians in the Black Power–inspired Black Arts Movement. "I was pretty popular at the time in the community because [my band] was doing a lot of cultural and political things through the music," Tony said. He was at first reluctant to become the director of the Afro-American Cultural Center because he did not think he had the necessary skills. However, he changed his mind after several friends persuaded him that he was qualified. "I decided to take the job on, and that's where I was purged through the fire," he said.

Many high school students across the United States also embraced Black Power. One of them was Zakiya Somburu. She was born in 1951 in Montclair, New Jersey, the oldest of two daughters. The family later moved to Newark, where, Zakiya said, she saw inequities in the school system: "The school I went to looked like a prison. It was very old. It had old desks with ink wells." When she was eight, her father died. Zakiya, her mother, and her sister then moved to East Orange, New Jersey, where the family had several relatives. "I grew up in a very loving, caring, nurturing home, enjoying it with extended family members. I know the critical value of extended family and support." In East Orange, Zakiya also experienced the contrast between urban and suburban schools. Her elementary school in suburban East Orange had fewer students and better facilities than the school she had attended in Newark. In the early 1960s, Zakiya said her mother wanted "an absolute change of scenery," so the family moved to San Francisco where her mother had siblings. In August 1965, when Zakiya was fourteen, her family left San Francisco to move back to East Orange. On their way, they drove to Los Angeles to pick up some relatives. At the time, the rebellion had broken out.

"I will always remember the violence, the powerlessness I felt," Zakiya recalled. "We were in a situation . . . like we were under siege. It was a war zone. . . . This was the first time I had ever seen guns drawn. [The National Guard] came to the apartment complex where we were living, and they kicked in the door with rifles drawn. They were looking for stolen property everywhere. I was terrified. . . . I didn't really have a political understanding about what was happening. I just felt that we were being attacked, and I was feeling like maybe we were going to die."

By the time Zakiya returned to East Orange to attend high school, like other many other Black youths of her age she had started reading books about Black history. "Many of us were very young but we all had a sense that this society was not right for us [Blacks], and we had to make it right," Zakiya said. "My mother always talked about education. . . . Her children must be educated, and so reading was a way for me to better understand what was going on and then try to get involved." At East Orange High School, she helped to start a Black Student Union.

The racial separatist beliefs espoused by Elijah Muhammad, leader of the Nation of Islam, gained the support of many Black people in the United States while Malcolm X was the national spokesperson for the organization. One group influenced by the teachings of Muhammad was the Republic of New Afrika (RNA), founded in Detroit in 1968 by Milton Henry (Gaidi Obadele), a Yale-educated Black attorney, and his brother Richard (Imari Abubakari Obadele). Like the Black Topographical Research Center, with which the RNA had close ties, the RNA then, as now, seeks the creation of an independent Black nation in North America.

The efforts of the Henry brothers and the RNA to start building the all-Black nation in Mississippi gained support from Robin David Parker. He was born in 1949 in America's "cereal capital," Battle Creek, Michigan, an only child whose mother nicknamed him "Che." He spent part of his childhood in Detroit before moving with his mother to Grand Rapids, Michigan, in the early 1960s after his parents separated. His political activism was inspired by his mother, a light-skinned African American woman who was active in the NAACP, Che said. "She had been accused of crossing over, of being half white and half mulatto. She was constantly having to support being Black. She said that regardless of how light she was or how fair her hair was, white folks still treated her like a 'nigger.'" After four Black girls were murdered in the bombing of a Black church in Birmingham, Alabama, in September 1963, civil rights groups in Grand Rapids held a protest march in which Che and his mother participated. "Shortly after that, we began having problems with the telephone," Che said. "My mother had been writing letters to the editor fairly regularly" about racial discrimination.

Che was active in the junior league of the Grand Rapids NAACP chapter, serving as president and a recruiter for the group throughout his high school years. When his mother remarried, Che said, the family was one of the first Black families to move to the predominantly white east side of Grand Rapids. Che was one of several Black students who integrated Ottawa High School in the mid-1960s after South High School, the Black high school, was closed and Grand Rapids instituted a busing program. To Che, the closing of

South High School was "catastrophic." At the time, he said, "There was an awful lot of Black unemployment. [Blacks] felt that the Dutch (white) population was kind of waving a stick in our faces and saying, 'All right. We're breaking up your schools, and your mothers and dads aren't going to have jobs.' The summers of 1965 and 1966 were really kind of testy."

At Ottawa High School, his fair skin color caused him to have trouble with white and Black students, Che said. "I laugh now when I think back on the white kids waiting for [the Black kids] after school to beat us up because we were Black. The Black kids would beat me up for being part 'yellow.' I really got the rock in the hard place. [My skin color] was a stigma, and I think that's probably what prompted me to be as intense in my struggle as I was. I've never dated a white woman and [didn't do] all that stereotypical stuff that goes along with having fair skin. I could convince the Black people that I was still on this [Black] side of the tracks as opposed to the other [white] side."

By the onset of the Black Power era in 1965, The Woodlawn Organization (TWO) had been active for several years organizing the predominantly Black residents of Chicago's South Side Woodlawn community. One of the many churches affiliated with the TWO was Christ Church Woodlawn, an Episcopalian church whose pastor was Father Earl A. Neil. He was born in 1935 in St. Paul, Minnesota, a child of activist parents who belonged to the local NAACP and the National Urban League. "The seed . . . of my commitment against injustice . . . my first memory, was planted when I was seven years old," Father Neil said. "My mother had us out on the picket line dealing with some school issues." Explaining more about how his Black consciousness was forged, he added: "In Minnesota, even to this day, there is just a handful of Black folk. A lot of Black people from large urban areas like New York City would say, 'What did you all [in Minnesota] know about racism or segregation?' Well, we knew a lot about it because as soon as we stepped out of the door, we were thrown up against white people as opposed to a larger city like Harlem, where you have a buffer of Black folk that you live with so that you may not see white folk for a while." Father Neil learned about segregation from the experiences of his father, who worked in a segregated group of Black firefighters. "When they desegregated [the fire department], that's when the whole issue of 'nigger beds' came up, because white firefighters didn't want to sleep in the same beds that Black firefighters slept in," Father Neil recalled.

He graduated from Carleton College in Minnesota in 1957, the first African American to do so in a four-year period, Father Neil said. He went on to earn his divinity degree from the Episcopalian Church's Seabury-Western Theological Seminary in 1960. After being pastor of a church in Wichita, Kansas, he served Christ Church Woodlawn from 1964 to 1967 and became active in TWO. The organization was created by several South Side Chicago churches and neighborhood organizations and was affiliated with labor leader Saul Alinsky's Industrial Areas Foundation. "There was a heavy involvement of the churches in various issues in Chicago at the time, and I found it to be an energizing and exciting time. My commitment was heightened when I was dealing with racism in the structure of the Episcopalian Church," Father Neil said. His involvement with TWO would put him in the heart of confrontational politics in Chicago during the early years of the Black Power era.

Beginning in the 1950s, the armed struggles of Blacks in Africa to win political independence from European colonialists was a source of inspiration to young Black activists in America's southern civil rights movement. One channel for African American activists to support the liberation struggles in Southern Africa was through the African Liberation Support Committee (ALSC). A major annual event of ALSC was African Liberation Day (ALD), held near May 19, the birthday of Malcolm X, and celebrated by people in Africa, the Caribbean, Latin America, and the United States.

Tanya Russell was the leader of an early ALD committee in San Francisco. Born in 1938 in Berkeley, Tanya was a "red diaper baby." Her father was a member of the Communist Party USA, and her mother had "passed through" the Young Communist League, Tanya said. Race became an issue for her at age five when, after her parents' divorce, her father married a white woman. "I saw them once a year." After graduating in 1959 from the University of California, Berkeley, where she studied to be a probation officer, Tanya moved to New York City in 1960 to join her fiancé. Following their marriage, their daughter was born in 1961.

Tanya worked with abused children in New York City. Her husband was a writer, and they helped to start a short-lived Black magazine, *Onyx*, to address "the burning questions" concerning Black people, Tanya said. The couple associated with Black people in New York City "who were promoting being proud of their looks," Tanya recalled. "I had a natural in 1960 that no one around me had. People would stop me on the subway and say, 'Why did you come outside with your hair like that, girl?' My husband had told me I would look good like that, and that was all I needed."

She and her husband admired Malcolm X, and the couple was prepared to join forces with Malcolm in 1964 after he left the Nation of Islam, an organization that Tanya considered oppressive to women. “Malcolm was so astute at articulating the essence of the problem even while he was still connected to the Nation,” Tanya said. “We would always go to the mosque when he spoke. It was the high point of my life.” Malcolm’s assassination in February 1965 prevented the Russells from carrying out their plan, and Tanya never joined any groups in New York City, she said. “When I look back at that time, [I did] a lot of intellectual maneuvering so I didn’t have to do anything. [I would say], ‘there’s a weakness here, there’s a weakness there,’ in an organization.” By 1969, her marriage had ended, and, with her young daughter, Tanya returned to Berkeley. There she became part of a network of Bay Area Black activists with connections to the ALSC and the ALD committee in Greensboro, North Carolina.

CHAPTER 3

Raising the Consciousness of the People

The Black Panther Intercommunal News Service, 1967–1980

The Death of Huey P. Newton

I was headed out the door to my job as managing editor of *Black Scholar* magazine in Oakland, when my phone rang the morning of Tuesday, August 22, 1989. The caller, a sister who had been a fellow BPP member in Oakland after first working for the party in Houston, rushed out the words: "JoNina, have you heard? Huey's been shot. He's dead." She explained that a friend in Oakland had heard the news and called to tell her.

Shocked, I had barely hung up the phone when it rang again. On the other end was another comrade sister (in the party, women were "comrade sisters" and men "comrade brothers") calling to ask if I had heard that Huey had been killed. "I miss him already," she said.

Grief overcame me as I realized that Huey P. Newton, whose name thousands across the world once chanted in the cry "Free Huey!" and who had been an international symbol of Black resistance to white oppression, was dead. Violence had consumed Huey's life almost daily in the twenty-three years since he cofounded the Black Panther Party, and violence finally took his life at age forty-seven.

The following Monday afternoon, August 28, at Huey's funeral, inside and outside East Oakland's Allen Temple Baptist Church, over two thousand people—including ex-Panthers from Baltimore, Boston, Houston, Detroit, Los Angeles, DC, Philadelphia, and other places—mourned Huey's death and celebrated the enduring contributions that the Panther leader and the party made to the political empowerment of Black and other disenfranchised people in the United States.

I was asked to speak at the funeral because I was an editor—the last editor—of the *Black Panther Intercommunal News Service*, the BPP's newspaper. As I stood crunched in line waiting to enter the sanctuary with Huey's family members and other speakers on the program—including former party leaders Bobby Seale, Elaine Brown, Ericka Huggins, David Hilliard, and Emory Douglas—I found myself looking into the faces of two Panther comrades whom I had not seen in fifteen years. We embraced—sad for the occasion that had reunited us but happy to be reunited.

When I stood on the podium to speak, I nearly broke down and cried as I looked into the faces of my Panther comrades on the front pews. I thought about all the good and hard times we had gone through together "serving the people body and soul." I said that I had been privileged to serve in the Black Panther Party for nine years and that I would die a Panther. I know I said something else, but I don't remember what.

When Elaine Brown took the podium, it was the first time many ex-Panthers and party supporters had seen her since 1977, when she resigned from the party for personal reasons. Her capable leadership held the BPP together from 1974 to 1977, when Huey was in exile in Cuba after being charged with killing an Oakland prostitute. He had survived being shot by one policeman, three years of prison for killing another policeman in the same incident, other confrontations with law enforcement, and numerous trials. In her comments, Elaine said she had thought Huey was invincible and that he would live forever.

Moving to the podium and putting a black beret on his head (in the party's early days, the Panther uniform consisted of a black beret, black leather jacket, and powder blue shirt), BPP cofounder and chair Bobby Seale brought the congregation to its feet in tribute when he raised his clenched fist and shouted the Panther rallying cry: "All power to the people!" Then he recalled how he and Huey met as students at Merritt College in the early 1960s, and how their mutual concerns about police brutality, poverty, and other problems in the Black community led them to found the BPP in Oakland in October 1966.

Just as he had in the old days, in his familiar strident cadence, Bobby then recited from memory the entire BPP Ten-Point Platform and Program. For a few minutes, it seemed as if the congregation at Allen Temple Church was at a Panther rally in 1968.

After the funeral, ex-Panthers, family members, and friends gathered for a reunion where we talked over old times and exchanged information about our lives since party days.

Later that afternoon, ex-BPP political prisoner Johnny Spain and I were among the guests on a program commemorating the legacy of the BPP on KPFA, the public radio station in Berkeley. Johnny, who spent nearly twenty-two consecutive years behind bars, explained how in the late 1960s, while serving a prison sentence for murder in

California, he joined the BPP because of his friendship with Black prison leader George Jackson.

Murder Linked to Death of George Jackson

George was legendary in the California penal system for his effective organizing of Black and poor inmates. He is generally credited with starting the Black Guerrilla Family (BGF). BGF was initiated as protection for Black inmates against white racist inmates and subsequently focused on political education for Black prisoners. During Huey's three-year imprisonment for killing an Oakland policeman, he learned of George's work and appointed him to the position of BPP field marshal, responsible for organizing and leading Blacks in prison. Many BGF members became Panthers.

On August 21, 1971, George, two other prisoners, and two guards were killed in San Quentin Prison's maximum-security section, "the adjustment center," in what prison officials alleged was an escape attempt. Earlier in the day during a visit, the officials charged, a white attorney, Stephen Bingham, had smuggled in a gun, concealed in a portable tape recorder, and an Afro wig. During George's escape attempt, they maintained, he concealed the gun under the wig. This theory was questionable, given that George was thoroughly searched before and after visits from his attorneys, family, and friends.

Johnny Spain was incarcerated at the time with George in the adjustment center. He and five other Black and Hispanic adjustment-center inmates—Willie Tate, Fleeta Drumgo, David Johnson, Luis Talamentez, and Hugo Pinell—were charged with assault, conspiracy, and murder in the August 21 killings. During the eighteen-month "San Quentin 6" trial, the prosecution conceded that Johnny did not kill anyone at the adjustment center but maintained that he was trying to escape with George. He was, therefore, vicariously guilty under state law of killing the two guards. When the trial ended in August 1976, almost exactly five years after the incident, Johnny was the only one of the six convicted of murder. He was sentenced to two consecutive life prison terms. In August 1989, shortly before Huey's murder, Johnny's conviction was overturned.

What really happened at San Quentin that August day forty years ago may never be revealed. In an affidavit signed shortly after the incident, several adjustment-center prisoners declared that George risked his life to save theirs. At the time of his death, the twenty-nine-year-old prison leader was serving the eleventh year of a $70 robbery conviction and was about to go on trial with two other Black inmates for the 1970 killing of a white guard at Soledad Prison. In his critically acclaimed 1970 book *Soledad Brother: The Prison Letters of George Jackson*—in part a forceful critique of racist violence and harassment of Black prisoners—George said he did not expect to leave prison alive because of his organizing of Black inmates. Aware of this and determined to silence him, prison officials may have falsely led George and inmates close to him to believe that the BPP was going to break him out of prison. The party denied the rumor that it had been organizing a prison escape and charged that prison officials murdered George, a charge supported by testimony during the San Quentin 6 trial. Louis Tackwood, a Black ex–police informant, testified that he was recruited to infiltrate the BPP as part of a plot by California law enforcement officials to kill George.

In any case, when George was killed, many in the BGF blamed the party, Huey in particular, and relations between the groups soured. Exactly eighteen years and one day later, Huey was shot to death on a street in the same Oakland neighborhood where Huey and Bobby launched the party in 1966. Tyrone Robinson, who police said was a drug dealer, was convicted on October 9, 1991, for the first-degree murder of Huey. According to police, Robinson said he shot Huey in a dispute over drugs. Robinson was a low-level member of the Black Guerrilla Family, police said, and killed Huey to advance in BGF ranks. For whatever reason Robinson killed Huey, there is no question that at the time of his death, the BGF was not the same organization that George Jackson founded twenty-two years earlier (when Robinson was a toddler). And there is also no doubt that by 1968, three years before George was killed, then–FBI director J. Edgar Hoover had already declared war on the BPP, charging that it was "the greatest threat to the internal security of the country."

Black Panther Party Founded to Oppose Police Brutality

Waiting to begin the KPFA program, and feeling more relaxed after the funeral celebration and more reflective from the emotions of the occasion, Johnny and I laughed at the headlines as we passed around twenty-year-old issues of the *Black Panther*:

NATIONWIDE HARASSMENT OF PANTHERS BY PIG POWER STRUCTURE

FASCIST ACTION AGAINST THE PEOPLE OF SACRAMENTO

WHITE 'MOTHER COUNTRY' RADICALS

During the program, while discussing the history of the newspaper and the party, I said that I owed Huey and Bobby a great debt for starting the BPP and allowing me to participate in one of the most important Black liberation movements in US history. As we reminisced, I recalled the party's beginnings in 1966 and my own introduction to the party six years later.

Huey and Bobby founded the Black Panther Party for Self-Defense because, as they later wrote in the party's initial Ten-Point Platform and Program, "We want freedom. We want power to determine the destiny of our Black Community."

The idea for the party's name came from a Black self-defense group in Lowndes County, Alabama, which used a black panther as its symbol. The panther is known as an animal that only attacks in self-defense. ("For Self-Defense" was dropped from the name of the party in 1968 to help give it legitimacy as a political organization.)

The two young men belonged to the community of southern Blacks whose families had migrated to Oakland during and after World War II in search of jobs in the naval shipyards and other industries. Huey's family came from Louisiana and Bobby's from Texas. Trying to escape the rigid segregation of the South, these Blacks became victims nonetheless of California-style discrimination—on the job, in housing, and in education. In addition, by the mid-1960s, the Oakland Police Department had recruited several white officers from the South who brought their racist attitudes with them. Police brutality in Oakland's Black communities was rampant.

Huey and Bobby formed the BPP partly as a response to the rise of white police brutality—which was occurring not only in Oakland but also in urban Black communities across America—and partly because they believed, as did many Black youth at the time, that the tactic of nonviolence successfully used by the civil rights movement in the South would not be effective in the large cities of the urban North.

At the time, it was legal for a person to carry an unconcealed gun in California. Point seven of the BPP platform called for "an immediate end to police brutality and murder of Black people" and advocated "organizing Black self-defense groups . . . dedicated to defending our Black community from racist police oppression and brutality." It said further, "The Second Amendment to the Constitution of the United States gives a right to bear arms. We therefore believe that all Black people should arm themselves for self-defense."

Huey, Bobby, and other Panthers conducted armed "community patrols of the police," during which they would observe police arrests and harassment of Blacks and advise those arrested or harassed of their legal rights. Huey became famous (or infamous, depending on one's perspective) for standing on street corners, armed with his gun, quoting citizens' rights from a law book as outraged police looked on.

White Power Structure Responds

The Black community had mixed reactions to gun-toting Panthers. Many—like me, initially—thought they were crazy and would get themselves and innocent bystanders killed. Others believed that Blacks had no recourse other than to arm ourselves against mounting police brutality.

The white power structure was less divided. To them, the sight of armed Black men was terrifying. Some whites may have been reminded of slave revolts and slaves who joined the Union army during the Civil War. The California power structure under the leadership of then-governor Ronald Reagan struck back. Legislation aimed at disarming the BPP, known as the Mulford Bill, was authored and proposed by East Bay legislator Don Mulford. The bill sought to change existing law by making it illegal for an unlicensed person to carry a loaded gun, concealed or unconcealed, in a public place.

On May 2, 1967, an armed contingent of Panthers led by Bobby Seale marched into the California legislature in Sacramento to protest the Mulford Bill. Later, on the steps of the state capitol, Bobby read the party's statement protesting the bill, "Executive Mandate No. 1," later published in the *Black Panther*.

> The Black Panther Party for Self-Defense calls upon the American people in general and the Black people in particular to take careful note of the racist California Legislature, which is now considering legislation aimed at keeping the Black people disarmed and powerless at the very same time that racist police agencies throughout the country are intensifying the terror, brutality, murder and repression of Black people.
>
> At the same time that the American government is waging a racist war of genocide in Vietnam, the concentration camps in which Japanese Americans were

interned during World War II are being renovated and expanded. Since America has historically reserved the most barbaric treatment for nonwhite people, we are forced to conclude that these concentration camps are being prepared for Black people, who are determined to gain their freedom by any means necessary. The enslavement of Black people from the very beginning of this country, the genocide practiced on the American Indians and the confining of the survivors on reservations, the savage lynching of thousands of Black men and women, the dropping of atomic bombs on Hiroshima and Nagasaki, and now the cowardly massacre in Vietnam, all testify to the fact that toward people of color the racist power structure of America has but one policy: repression, genocide, terror and the big stick.

Black people have begged, prayed, petitioned, demonstrated and everything else to get the racist power structure of America to right the wrongs which have historically been perpetrated against Black people. All of these efforts have been answered by more repression, deceit, and hypocrisy. As the aggression of the racist American government escalates in Vietnam, the police agencies of America [escalate] the repression of Black people throughout the ghettos of America. Vicious police dogs, cattle prods and increased patrols have become familiar sights in Black communities. City Hall turns a deaf ear to the pleas of Black people for relief from this increasing terror.

The Black Panther Party for Self-Defense believes that the time has come for Black people to arm themselves against this terror before it is too late. The

> pending Mulford Act brings the hour of doom one step nearer. A people who have suffered so much for so long at the hands of a racist society, must draw the line somewhere. We believe that the Black communities of America must rise up as one man to halt the progression of a trend that leads inevitably to their total destruction.

The Mulford Bill was later passed.

Nearing the end of my freshman year at Baker University in Baldwin, Kansas, I saw the televised footage of armed Panthers marching into the California legislature. The BPP, which had been a local group until then, gained national attention, and Panther chapters began to appear in major cities across the country.

Hoover Begins Infiltration Program

Unlike the Mulford Bill, other attacks on the party were not so overt or legal. "War against the Panthers: A Study of Repression in America," Huey's 1980 doctoral dissertation at the University of California, Santa Cruz, is a detailed account of the government's harassment of the BPP—which was dominated by the FBI's COINTELPRO. On August 25, 1967, FBI records show, the FBI launched a violent and illegal program to destroy the Black liberation movement in America. In a memo, Hoover ordered forty-one FBI field offices to "expose, disrupt, misdirect, discredit, or otherwise neutralize the activities of black nationalist . . . hate-type organizations and groupings, their leadership, spokesmen, membership and supporters."

Initial groups targeted were SNCC, SCLC, CORE, the Nation of Islam, and the Revolutionary Action Movement. The BPP was added to the list in September 1968.

At Hoover's direction, FBI offices across the country planted spies and informants in the BPP and other Black radical and civil rights groups in the sixties and seventies to destroy them from within. COINTELPRO was also used against Native American, Chicano, Asian, and white leftist groups during this period.

COINTELPRO operations against the BPP were varied and vicious, and they included hundreds of false arrests. From January 1, 1968, to December 31, 1969, 739 BPP members were arrested, an average of more than one a day, resulting in close to $5 million spent on bail. One FBI tactic was securing respected establishment journalists to write negative articles about the BPP. Another was to send anonymous letters to churches whose facilities the party used for the free breakfast program, letters falsely accusing Panthers of teaching Black children to hate whites.

By July 1969, the BPP was the primary target of the "black nationalist" subset of COINTELPRO. Ultimately, 233 of the 295 authorized "black nationalist" actions had been carried out against the BPP. At least twenty-eight Panthers were killed as a result.

The worst of the COINTELPRO activities against the party was the planting of undercover informants, usually Black, in party affiliates. A paid FBI informant in Chicago, William O'Neal, provided information that led to the murders by police of Illinois Panther leaders Fred Hampton and Mark Clark on December 4, 1969, in the westside Chicago apartment that was used as the local BPP headquarters. Fred, a brilliant, charismatic leader who built the Chicago

BPP chapter into one of the largest and most successful in the country, was shot to death while asleep in bed, probably drugged by O'Neal. (After living under an assumed identity for twenty years after these events, O'Neal committed suicide in January 1990.)

Details of COINTELPRO operations against the BPP were published in the April 1976 final report of the US Senate Committee to Study Governmental Operations with Respect to Intelligence Activities, known as the Church Committee after its chair, Frank Church, a Democratic senator from Idaho who served from 1957 to 1981. The introduction to the 989-page report concluded: "Many of the techniques used would be intolerable in a democratic society even if all targets had been involved in violent activity, but COINTELPRO went far beyond that. The unexpressed major premise of the programs was that a law enforcement agency has the duty to do whatever is necessary to combat perceived threats to the existing social and political order."

Accusing the FBI of inciting violence between Panthers and other groups, the Church Committee declared, "It is deplorable that officials of the United States government should engage in the activities described below . . . equally disturbing is the pride which those officials took in claiming credit for the bloodshed that occurred."

First *Black Panther* Focuses on Denzil Dowell Killing

The first issue of the *Black Panther Black Community News Service*, a four-page mimeographed sheet published April 25, 1967, focused on the killing of Denzil Dowell, a twenty-two-year-old Black man, by a white sheriff's deputy in Richmond, California. According to the official police report, Dowell was killed after he fled from the deputy, who had stopped Dowell and ordered him to show his identification. Dowell's family disputed the police account and charged that he was murdered. Residents of the area where Dowell was killed said they heard six to ten shots fired. The coroner's report said there were six to ten bullet wounds in Dowell's body, but the police said only three shots were fired. Police said Dowell jumped over a fence during their pursuit of him. Family members said a hip injury he received in a car accident some time earlier made it impossible for Dowell to jump over a fence. They also charged that the deputy who killed Dowell knew him and had previously threatened to kill him.

The family of Dowell asked the fledgling BPP to investigate the young Black man's killing, which was ruled justifiable homicide. The combative editorial of the inaugural *Black Panther* set the paper's tone for the next four years. After listing "questionable facts" about the killing raised by Dowell's family, the newspaper said, "The white cop is the instrument sent into our community by the Power Structure to keep Black People quiet and under control. . . . It is time that Black People start moving in a direction that will free our communities from this form of outright brutal oppression. The Black Panther Party for Self-Defense has worked out a program that is carefully designed to cope with this situation."

Former BPP "revolutionary artist" and minister of culture Emory Douglas coordinated layout and design of the *Black Panther* from the second issue of the paper until the last one in October 1980. In a March 1991 interview, he recalled the early days of the *Black Panther*. "Huey compared the party's need for a publication with the armed struggle of the Vietnamese people that was going on at that time," Emory said. "He said that the Vietnamese carried mimeograph machines wherever they went to produce flyers and other literature to spread the word about their fight to free their country. The party needed to have a newspaper so we could tell our own story."

Eldridge Cleaver Becomes First Editor

Eldridge Cleaver, one of the BPP's most controversial leaders, was the first editor of the *Black Panther*. In December 1966, only five months before the first issue came out, he had been paroled from prison after gaining national recognition for *Soul on Ice*, his treatise on how being an oppressed Black man in America led him to be a rapist. At Huey's invitation, he joined the party in 1967 after a BPP confrontation with police at the Berkeley office of *Ramparts* magazine, a white leftist publication. Eldridge was married to the former Kathleen Neal, who became BPP communications secretary and a well-known party spokesperson. Kathleen had been an activist in Nashville in SNCC, and in June 1967 a short-lived merger of the BPP and SNCC began.

Huey believed that the party could become more adept at community organizing using the tactics SNCC had successfully employed in the South. In "Executive Mandate No. 2," published in the July 3, 1967, *Black Panther* (vol. 1, no. 4), the BPP "drafted" SNCC leader Stokely Carmichael (now known as Kwame Ture) into the party with the rank of field marshal.

So Let This Be Heard . . .

Brother Stokely Carmichael:

Because you have distinguished yourself in the struggle for the total liberation of Black People from oppression in racist white America;

Because you have acted courageously and shown great fortitude under the most adverse circumstances;

Because you have proven yourself as a true revolutionary guided by a great feeling of love for our people;

Because you have set such a fine example, in the tradition of Brother Malcolm, of dedicating your entire life to the struggle of Black Liberation, inspiring our youth and providing a model for others to emulate;

Because you have refused to serve in the oppressor's racist mercenary aggressive war machine, showing that you know who your true friends and enemies are;

Because of your new endeavor to organize and liberate the Crown Colony of Washington DC, you will inevitably be forced to confront, deal with, and conquer the racist Washington Police Department which functions as the protector of the racist dog power structure, occupying the Black Community in the same manner and for the same reasons that the racist U. S. Armed Forces occupy South Vietnam;

You are hereby drafted into the Black Panther Party for Self-Defense, invested with the rank of Field Marshall, delegated the following authority, power and responsibility:

To establish revolutionary law, order, and justice in the territory lying between the Continental Divide East to the Atlantic Ocean; North of the Mason-Dixon Line

to the Canadian Border; South of the Mason-Dixon Line to the Gulf of Mexico.
. . . So Let It Be Done

The alliance was formalized at a "Free Huey Rally" in Oakland on February 17, 1968, the twenty-sixth birthday of the incarcerated BPP cofounder.

"Eldridge was a flamboyant person in those days, and his writing was provocative," Emory said in characterizing the *Black Panther*'s content under its first editor. Huey, Bobby, and other party members contributed ideas and articles to the paper. The newspaper also included articles from people in the community, a practice that continued throughout the paper's existence. Members of BPP chapters throughout the country wrote articles to report news and issues in their local areas.

When Eldridge first became editor, the paper was produced at the home of his attorney, Beverly Axelrod, Emory said. Later, production moved to the apartment where Eldridge and Kathleen lived in San Francisco. Production also took place at the homes of other party members who lived in the city.

The first two issues of the *Black Panther* were done on a mimeograph machine. Afterward, the newspaper was typed, and graphics were done with instant type. Rubber cement was used to paste the galleys down. Kathleen and other BPP members typed and proofread articles.

Beginning with the third issue, Emory began to oversee the paper's format. "My job was to make the paper look appealing and to see that the artwork was in line with the party's politics," he said. Under Emory's leadership, the newspaper's layout cadre used creative designs that most

Black newspapers had not widely used at the time. The front page of the *Black Panther* had a magazine flavor.

Emory Douglas: Revolutionary Artist

Emory would later outline his views as a revolutionary artist in a speech at Fisk University in Nashville in October 1972. In the speech, which was printed in the *Black Panther*, the artist said:

> If we take this structure of commercial art and add a brand new content to it, then we will begin to analyze Black people and our situation for the purpose of raising our consciousness to the oppression that we are subjected to. We would use commercial art for the purpose of educating Black people. . . . No artist can sit in an ivory tower, discussing the problems of the day, and come up with a solution on a piece of paper. The artist has to be down on the ground; he has to hear the sounds of the people, the cries of the people, the suffering of the people, the laughter of the people—the dark side and the bright side of our lives. . . . We must understand that when there are over twenty million people in this country, hungry, then we, as artists, have something we must deal with.

When the party opened an office on Shattuck Avenue in Berkeley, a Justifax machine and later a Compugraphic machine were used for typesetting. Throughout the thirteen years of its production, the *Black Panther* was typeset at party offices by BPP members or others hired by the party.

Newspaper distribution was a party-wide activity. In 1967, Emory distributed the *Black Panther* in his hometown of San Francisco, where he sold papers in the then predominantly Black communities of Fillmore and Hunter's Point. Huey, Bobby, Eldridge, and other BPP members would sell papers at their speaking engagements.

"Free Huey" Heard around the World

The BPP gained increased national attention and membership following the October 28, 1967, shooting incident involving Huey and two white Oakland police officers, Herbert Heanes and John Frey. The officers, who recognized the license plates of the car in which Huey was a passenger as that of a BPP vehicle, ordered the car to stop. In the bloody altercation that followed, Heanes was wounded, and Frey was killed. Huey, himself seriously wounded, was arrested for Frey's killing.

A picture of Huey lying wounded and handcuffed to a hospital gurney appeared on national TV and in newspapers. The BPP, charging that Heanes and Frey had tried to murder Huey, launched an international campaign to get the BPP minister of defense out of jail. "Free Huey," a frequent headline in the *Black Panther* at that time, became the demand of Black, white, and Third World progressive and radical groups around the world. As a result, hundreds of urban Black youths across America joined the party.

On September 8, 1968, Huey was convicted of manslaughter in Frey's death. Three weeks later, he was sentenced to two to fifteen years in prison and was imprisoned until his release on August 5, 1970, after his conviction was overturned.

In 1968 Sam Napier joined the BPP in San Francisco. He was the party's dedicated circulation manager until his murder in New York City in April 1971. "Sam had a great desire to distribute the paper. That's what he wanted to do," Emory said. Sam traveled all over the country securing distributors for the *Black Panther*. "He would call and tell us where he was and that he had gotten another route."

In the pages of the *Black Panther*, the BPP stated its views in speeches and writings by party leaders on "the correct handling of a revolution." In an article with that title published in the May 4, 1968, issue, Huey wrote, "The Vanguard Party must provide leadership for the people. It must teach the correct strategic methods of prolonged resistance through literature and activities. . . . When the people learn that it is no longer advantageous for them to resist by going to the streets in large numbers and when they see the advantage in the activities of guerrilla warfare methods, they will quickly follow this example."

It was also common for the newspaper to print articles written by Cuban president Fidel Castro, Chinese leader Mao Zedong, and the late Mozambican president Samora Machel.

"The paper gave Black, poor, and dispossessed people a grassroots point of view on the news that they had never had before," Emory said in assessing the contribution of the *Black Panther*.

Thanks to Emory and other artists like Mark Teemer and Matilaba (Joan Tarika Lewis), the first female member of the BPP, the *Black Panther* published artwork that most people had never seen before. The BPP's contributions to popular culture of the era included the verbal and visual depiction of police as pigs. The pig, because it is commonly thought of as a dirty animal, was chosen by the BPP as a symbol of police brutality in the Black community. Many people bought the newspaper just to see Emory's latest cartoons of pigs dressed in police uniforms, which could be found in almost every issue from 1967 to about 1970. *Black Panther: The Revolutionary Art of Emory Douglas*, published in 2007, is a collection of some of Emory's finest work and includes essays by former Panther leaders Bobby Seale and Kathleen Cleaver as well as actor Danny Glover.

In its early years, the paper printed the names of BPP national and local leaders, as well as addresses of recognized chapters and branches. While this practice helped people who needed assistance finding Panthers in their local communities, it also unfortunately helped the FBI and police to infiltrate the party with agents provocateurs, the lifeblood of Hoover's COINTELPRO.

Eldridge Goes into Exile

Two days after the April 4, 1968, assassination of Dr. Martin Luther King Jr., Bobby Hutton, the first BPP member and the party's seventeen-year-old treasurer, was shot to death by Oakland police as he walked out of a house, hands above his head, to surrender. Eldridge and six other Panthers, including chief of staff David Hilliard, were arrested on conspiracy and murder charges in connection with Bobby's death. Fearing that he would return to prison, in late 1968 Eldridge fled with Kathleen, first going to Cuba and eventually settling in Algiers, Algeria, where he became "underground" editor of the *Black Panther* and head of the BPP's newly established international section.

By this time, the BPP–SNCC merger had begun to fall apart. In an article in the March 31, 1969, issue of the *Black Panther*, Bobby Seale and the BPP minister of education Raymond "Masai" Hewitt criticized views expressed by Stokely during a visit to Scandinavian countries. Bobby charged that Stokely had "deviated from the party's political line." An article in the August 16, 1969, *Black Panther* reported that David Hilliard had recently met with Stokely in Algiers, and that it was unlikely that Stokely would continue as a party member. Writing from Algiers, in an "Open Letter to Stokely Carmichael" (*Black Panther*, August 16, 1969), Eldridge attacked Stokely's "Black Power" philosophy: "There is not going to be any revolution or Black liberation in the United States as long as revolutionary Blacks, whites, Mexicans, Puerto Ricans, Indians, Chinese and Eskimos are unwilling to unite in some functional machinery that can cope with this situation [capitalism, imperialism, and racism]."

Back in the United States, changes were made in the editorial staff of the *Black Panther*. After Eldridge went into exile, Raymond Lewis became managing editor of the *Black Panther* and deputy minister of information. By January 1969, Frank Jones had replaced Lewis. In March, Elbert "Big Man" Howard and Bobby Herron became coeditors of the newspaper. By the end of March, Big Man replaced Frank Jones as managing editor.

During Eldridge's tenure as BPP minister of information, which ended in February 1971, he encouraged a free speech movement in the party. Public statements by party leaders and the newspaper were filled with profanity. Although the profanity may have reflected the language of some activists of the period, it may also have offended some readers.

Newspaper sales declined, according to Emory. "We did a great disservice to the party and the people in the community," he said of the free speech movement. Huey, from prison, criticized it sharply, and it was eventually stopped. While Huey did not regularly oversee the format and contents of the newspaper, even when he was not imprisoned, if he wanted particular information included, his wishes were carried out, as they were in this case.

Even after his tenure as editor ended, Eldridge remained famous for his colorful speeches and writings, often filled with expletives castigating the US power structure. In one article published in the November 22, 1969, issue of the *Black Panther*, he declared: "A dead pig is desirable, but a paralyzed pig is preferable to a mobile pig. And a determined revolutionary doesn't require an authorization from a Central Committee [BPP leadership body] before offing a pig . . . when the need arises a true revolutionary will off the Central Committee. In order to stop the slaughter of the people we accelerate the slaughter of the pigs."

"One of the Most Effective Propaganda Operations"

The writings and speeches of Eldridge, Huey, Bobby Seale, and other BPP leaders that appeared in the *Black Panther* came under close government scrutiny at this time. On October 8, 1969, the Committee on Internal Security of the US House of Representatives, chaired by Missouri congressman Richard H. Ichord, authorized an investigation into "the origin, history, organization, character, and objectives" of the BPP as reported in the *Black Panther*. A year later, on October 6, 1970, the committee issued its report of about 150 pages detailing the newspaper's contents from June 1967 to September 1970. The report included excerpts from *Black Panther* articles, cartoons, and photos of party leaders.

For the BPP, 1970 was a critical year. In a memo of May 15, Hoover described the *Black Panther* as "one of the most effective propaganda operations of the BPP," adding, "It is the voice of the BPP and if it could be effectively hindered it would result in helping to cripple the BPP." Certainly, Hoover had cause for concern. The *Black Panther* had arguably become one of the most popular and colorful radical-left publications of the era. At twenty-five cents per copy, the *Black Panther*'s weekly circulation had surpassed 100,000. Subscriptions and contributors came from around the world, including France, Sweden, Denmark, England, Japan, China, North Korea, Mozambique, Guinea-Bissau, and Cuba. Of such "alternative" publications, only *Muhammad Speaks*, the newspaper of the Nation of Islam, was selling more copies.

Less than a week after Hoover's memo ordering FBI field offices to "cripple" the BPP, the San Diego FBI office proposed to spray a foul-smelling chemical called Skatole on copies of the *Black Panther*. In June, FBI headquarters concocted a plan to "ignite the fuel of conflict" between the BPP and the Nation of Islam by reducing sales of *Muhammad Speaks*. However, in July, the Chicago field office advised against pursuing this project, warning that, due to existing tensions between the two groups, "any revelation of a Bureau attempt to encourage conflict might serve to bring the BPP and NOI closer together."

In November 1970, FBI headquarters directed field offices to distribute copies of a column written by Victor Riesel, a white labor columnist, calling for a nationwide union boycott of handling the *Black Panther*, which was shipped around the country by air freight. The Church Committee could not determine the outcome of this plan.

FBI Plot Creates Rift between Huey and Eldridge

Earlier, in March 1970, the FBI had launched a COINTELPRO action to create a permanent rift between Huey and Eldridge. Each was isolated from the party—Eldridge in exile in Algeria and Huey in prison. Exploiting this situation, the Bureau sent an anonymous letter to Eldridge saying that BPP leaders in California were trying to undermine his influence. As a result of this fake letter, Eldridge expelled three members of the BPP's international section.

Pleased with the apparent success of the letter, the FBI followed it up with another one, to David Hilliard, written to appear as if it had come from Connie Matthews, the party's representative in Scandinavia. "[Eldridge] has tripped out," the letter said. "Perhaps he has been working too hard." The letter suggested that David "take some immediate action before this becomes more serious." In May 1970, Eldridge called BPP national headquarters in Oakland and talked to David, Connie, and other BPP leaders. Suspicion was expressed that the letters had probably been sent by the FBI or CIA.

Nevertheless, the FBI continued with its campaign to cause dissension between Huey and Eldridge. About a week after Huey's release from prison on August 5, 1970, an FBI informant in Philadelphia distributed a fake directive to local Panthers questioning Huey's leadership ability. The fictitious COINTELPRO letters to Huey and Eldridge, alleging that each was critical of the other's leadership, continued throughout the rest of 1970 and into early 1971, and they resulted in Huey's expulsion of several key members from the party, including Connie Matthews.

On February 26, 1971, during a TV interview, Eldridge criticized the expulsions and suggested that David Hilliard be removed as BPP chief of staff. As a result, Huey expelled Eldridge and the entire international section of the party. Their expulsions were reported in the March 6 edition of the *Black Panther*. The FBI program to create a permanent rift between Huey and Eldridge had succeeded.

In New York City, where animosity between the pro-Huey and pro-Eldridge groups was the greatest, several BPP members were expelled. In separate incidents there in March and April 1971, Panthers Sam Napier and Harold Russell were shot to death.

In his critical essay published in the April 17, 1971, issue of the *Black Panther*, "On the Defection of Eldridge Cleaver from the Black Panther Party and the Defection of the Black Panther Party from the Black Community," Huey wrote: "We recognize that nothing in nature stands outside of dialectics, even the Black Panther Party. But we welcome these contradictions, because they clarify our struggle. We had a contradiction with our former minister of information, Eldridge Cleaver. But we understand this as necessary to our growth."

While praising Eldridge for his "great contributions to the Black Panther Party with his writing and speaking," Huey accused him of joining the BPP for the wrong reasons: "Without my knowledge, he [Eldridge] took this [confrontation between Huey and the San Francisco Police in front of the *Ramparts* magazine office, where Eldridge worked] as *the* Revolution and *the* Party . . . the police confrontation left him fixated with the 'either-or' attitude. This was that either the community picked up the gun with the party or else they were cowards and there was no place for them." Criticizing the BPP for its free speech movement, which he said had isolated the party from the Black community, Huey said, "The Black Panther Party defected from the community long before Eldridge defected from the Party."

Paper Embraces "Intercommunal" Struggle

Two months earlier, in February, Huey had changed the full name of the newspaper from the *Black Panther Black Community News Service* to the *Black Panther Intercommunal News Service*. The change was made to reflect the party's shift from a largely Black-nationalist perspective to one advocating an international or "intercommunal" struggle against racism and imperialism that cut across all color lines.

Regular features of the newspaper at that time, in addition to the party's Ten-Point Platform and Program, included "People's Perspective," a column on national news events affecting Black and Third World people; "Black and Community News," including articles about party leaders, programs, and events; "Intercommunal News," which featured news about freedom movements in Southern Africa, Central America, and the Middle East; book excerpts and book and movie reviews; and a list of BPP "survival programs," such as the free breakfast program for schoolchildren, the free medical clinics, and the free food and legal aid programs. The *Black Panther* was circulated internationally. African liberation movements and many foreign embassies subscribed to it. It was also popular on college and university campuses.

Brown and Huggins Become Succeeding Editors

Succeeding *Black Panther* editors included Elaine Brown and Ericka Huggins. The two women and Ericka's husband, John, were early party members in the Los Angeles BPP chapter founded by deputy minister of defense Alprentice "Bunchy" Carter, a former gang leader who had served time in prison. On January 17, 1969, Bunchy and John, the chapter's minister of information, were shot to death during a meeting of Black students at the University of California, Los Angeles. Five members of United Slaves (US), the Black-nationalist organization founded by Maulana Karenga, were charged with killing the Southern California BPP leaders. Two of the five remained at large. The other three, brothers George and Larry Stiner and Claude Hubert, were convicted of murder. The Church Committee later revealed that COINTELPRO instigated and then perpetuated rising violence between the BPP and US by sending inflammatory letters to the rival groups, claiming each was out to destroy the other. In a *Penthouse* interview published in April 1979, "Othello," a former agent provocateur in the Los Angeles BPP, charged that the Stiners and Hubert were police informants in US.

Following the deaths of Bunchy and John, Elaine, who had been communications secretary for the Los Angeles BPP chapter, became its deputy minister of information, the number two post in a chapter. She went to Oakland around 1970 and became editor of the *Black Panther*. Her writing and editing skills greatly improved the quality and professionalism of the newspaper. However, in late 1972, Elaine's tenure as editor ended when she ran for Oakland City Council in a historic campaign with Bobby Seale, who ran for mayor. While the two BPP leaders lost the election in April 1973, they captured 40 percent of the vote, bolstering Black political power in Oakland and paving the way for the election of the city's first Black mayor, Lionel Wilson, in 1977. In 1975 Elaine was defeated in a close race in her second run for city council.

Ericka, while in New Haven, Connecticut, to bury her husband, was arrested and jailed for conspiracy and murder, along with seven other Panthers, in the May 1969 death of New York BPP member Alex Rackley. Ericka and Bobby Seale, who also was charged with Rackley's murder, stood trial together in a case that was regularly covered in the *Black Panther*. In late May 1971 the jury deadlocked, a mistrial was declared, and Ericka was released after two years behind bars. (Bobby, sentenced in November 1969 to four years in prison for contempt in the Chicago Eight trial, would not be released until 1972.) Moving to Oakland in 1971, Ericka followed Elaine as *Black Panther* editor, a position she held until about mid-1972. In 1973 Ericka became director of the Intercommunal Youth Institute (later renamed Oakland Community School), the BPP's award-winning, community-based elementary school.

David Du Bois Institutes Collective Decision Making

David G. Du Bois succeeded Ericka as editor of the *Black Panther*. During the summer of 1972, the stepson of W. E. B. Du Bois—the great African American historian and sociologist—returned to the United States following a thirteen-year absence. David had spent his time abroad working as a journalist and college professor in Egypt and Ghana and traveling in Africa, Europe, the Soviet Union, and the People's Republic of China, where he was a student for a time.

"When I came to the Black Panther Party, I was no spring chicken," David wrote in a 1990 letter. "I was forty-seven years old and had cut my revolutionary teeth on street demonstrations with other [World War II] war-weary GIs in the Philippines demanding our right to go home and in the East Coast student and veterans' movements of the mid and late 1940s." He became frustrated with the failure of these movements to "honestly and decisively" deal with issues impacting American Blacks. Thus, in 1959 David began his exile from the United States.

Back in America in 1972, David began to research the achievements of the civil rights movement of the 1960s, which had taken place during his absence. At the top of his list was the BPP. Many party leaders, including David Hilliard and Eldridge Cleaver, traveled in Africa during the late 1960s, and David Du Bois had met some of them in Cairo, Egypt, where he lived. "Through these contacts I learned firsthand much about the party. . . . Most of what I learned increased an already intense admiration for these young ghetto Blacks who had decided they had taken it long enough and were prepared to fight fire with fire," David wrote.

In November and December 1972, he visited the San Francisco Bay Area, where he finally met Huey and toured BPP programs in Oakland and Berkeley. Later, at a dinner with other party members, Huey shared with David his "fantasy" that David would become editor-in-chief of the *Black Panther*. David was a veteran journalist, and Huey was always concerned with improving the professionalism of the newspaper. Several days later, David began his three-year association with the BPP as editor of the party's newspaper. Huey insisted that David be a party employee, not a member, "making me, he hoped, less a target for the party's enemies," David recalled.

While assured by Huey that he would have complete freedom with the content and format of the *Black Panther*, David nevertheless began his work cautiously. Reflecting on his early days as editor of *BPINS*, as the paper was sometimes referred to by party members, David wrote, "The most serious initial challenge I faced was winning the confidence and the willing cooperation of the paper's staff. None had had formal journalistic training or newspaper experience, except that they had gained getting out the party paper. Their work methods had successfully produced the paper week after succeeding week. . . . 'So, who is this aging bourgeois outsider taking over and threatening changes?' they [newspaper staff] said to me with their eyes and in their manner toward me."

Being the stepson of W. E. B. Du Bois helped David's status with party members. Perhaps more important in helping him gradually win the staff's confidence, he insisted that the staff make collective decisions about the content and format of the paper. While weekly newspaper meetings were routine, David at first found it difficult to get staff members to express their opinions. With his encouragement, their reluctance abated in time, and they contributed ideas and opinions that continually improved the *Black Panther* and its status among BPP members.

In 1972 the *Black Panther* began a series of articles on sickle cell anemia. The rare blood disease mostly afflicts people of African descent, and for this reason, the party charged, medical science had made little effort to study the disease and develop a treatment for it. The party also launched a free, nationwide sickle cell anemia testing program.

Recruited to Detroit BPP Chapter

Meanwhile, the summer of 1972 was also eventful for me. My fiancé, Joe Abron, a Detroit native and Purdue University junior, joined the local chapter of the BPP. Having recently earned my master's degree in communication from Purdue, I worked in Chicago as public information officer at Malcolm X College and later as a reporter for the *Chicago Daily Defender*. Frequently I went to Detroit for weekends to visit Joe and to do party work. We both firmly believed that Black people who wanted to make social change needed to belong to an organization in order to have the greatest impact, so I soon followed him into the BPP.

By the time I joined the party, my views about the Black struggle had been shaped by the southern civil rights movement of the 1950s and early 1960s, which I observed at a distance during my childhood in Jefferson City, Missouri. I lived in the Missouri capital city with my parents and two younger sisters from 1953 to 1966. My father, J. Otis Erwin (1922–2003), a United Methodist minister, established the Wesley Foundation at Lincoln University and taught philosophy and religion at Lincoln, then a predominantly Black school. From him and my mother, Adeline Comer Erwin (1919–2019), who had been a college music teacher before marrying my father, I learned that Blacks with skills had a responsibility to use them to better the Black race.

Watching television and reading news accounts, I was impressed by the courage of Blacks and their white allies who often risked their lives to defy Jim Crow segregation laws in the South and demand the right of Blacks to vote and to attend the schools of their choice. In the summer of 1964, when Black and white students in SNCC and other civil rights groups launched a massive voter registration drive in Mississippi, I wanted to join them. My mother, however, told me it was much too dangerous for a sixteen-year-old girl like me to go to Mississippi.

At any rate, by the time I graduated from high school in May 1966, I had decided that whatever my career would be as an adult, I would use it to help Black people. I spent the next four years in college at Baker University in Baldwin, Kansas, where I majored in journalism. When Martin Luther King Jr. was assassinated on April 4, 1968, I was near the end of my sophomore year. Dr. King's murder troubled me deeply and strengthened my resolve to get involved in the Black movement.

That summer, I was one of six Baker students and two faculty members who spent eight weeks in the southern African country of Rhodesia, now Zimbabwe. Rhodesia was the first African country I had ever visited. My knowledge of Africa was so limited that I had assumed African Blacks controlled their countries. In Rhodesia, I learned that the country had been under British rule since the late nineteenth century, and that Blacks had launched an armed struggle to win their freedom. Living on a Methodist church mission, I worked for a Black newspaper that was regularly censored by the government for printing news critical of the white regime, which the US government supported. (Twenty-five years later, in 1983, I would take another study trip to Zimbabwe, whose Black-majority government had been in power for three years.) Returning to Baker with increased determination to work in the Black movement after graduation, I became coeditor of the campus newspaper, the *Baker Orange*, during my junior and senior years. After graduating in May 1970, I went to Purdue to graduate school.

Party Work in the Motor City

By the time I joined the BPP in the summer of 1972, the COINTELPRO campaign against the party had taken its toll on Detroit Panthers. Many members had resigned, and several were imprisoned, leaving less than a dozen members in the Motor City.

Afraid that a sheltered minister's daughter like me would not be accepted by streetwise party members, I began my apprenticeship as a would-be Panther selling the *Black Panther*. In platform shoes, I walked up and down endless drab hallways in Detroit housing projects, urging all who opened their doors to "Get your Black Panther news! Get your people's paper!" My Panther comrades and I had fun competing with Nation of Islam members for newspaper sales on Detroit streetcorners. For the most part, the competition was friendly and consisted of members of the two groups trying to outtalk each other for sales.

In August 1973, Joe and I were married. Four months later, in December 1973, he graduated from Purdue, and we returned to Detroit to work full time in the party. My main jobs were to work in the free breakfast for schoolchildren program; to drive for the free prison busing program, which provided transportation for relatives of prisoners to visit their loved ones at Michigan's Jackson State Prison; and to sell the *Black Panther*. I worked hard and earned the respect of my comrades.

I became a writer for the party's paper in early 1974 after moving to Oakland with Joe and other members of the Detroit BPP chapter. At the time, there were thirteen comrades in the newspaper cadre, as we were called, consisting of writers, led by editor David Du Bois, and layout staff (pasteup and typesetting), led by artist Emory Douglas. In a given week, writers might be assigned to cover a city council meeting, a community rally, or a speech by Bobby Seale or Elaine Brown. During my first few months there, I did a series on the party's alternative school, the Intercommunal Youth Institute.

In April 1974, shortly after my arrival in Oakland, local police raided a party facility on 29th Avenue in East Oakland where children from the Intercommunal Youth Institute often stayed. Several BPP members were arrested, and police seized party documents and files in the house. A few days later, while in a laundromat across the street from the apartment where I lived with Joe and other Panthers, I was approached by two white men who showed me badges identifying them as FBI agents.

"Hi, JoNina. We want to talk to you for a minute," one of the smiling agents said. "We know that you just came to Oakland to work with the Black Panthers. There's been trouble recently [referring to the 29th Avenue raid], and we don't think you want to be involved in that. Maybe we can help." His voice and manner were pleasant. Nevertheless, the familiar way he spoke, as if he knew all about me, terrified me. Panthers were trained never to talk to police without an attorney present. I told the FBI agents I had nothing to say to them and tore out of the laundromat back to my apartment, where I called party headquarters to tell them what had happened. I had experienced what I believe was a COINTELPRO action.

Crisis in 1974

Eight months after my arrival in Oakland, in August 1974, the party underwent another crisis. In separate incidents that month, police charged Huey with beating a Black tailor, Preston Callins, and shooting a Black prostitute, Kathleen Smith, to death. Afraid he might return to prison, Huey disappeared. A few weeks later, he surfaced in Havana, Cuba, where he lived in exile with his wife and Panther comrade, Gwen, for the next three years. The charges against Huey and his disappearance caused considerable confusion within party ranks and severely damaged our reputation in the community. Unsure of the party's future and weary from years of courtroom trials and police harassment, party chair Bobby Seale and several other BPP Central Committee members also disappeared. With Bobby gone, Huey, from Havana, gave leadership of the party to Elaine Brown and appointed her BPP chair.

As the party coped with the departure of its cofounders, the *Black Panther* continued its weekly publication schedule. Once again, "Free Huey!" became a recurring theme in the paper. Other articles in the paper at that time reflected the expansion of the party's work and influence under Elaine's tenure as party chair. The BPP worked with such diverse groups as the United Farmworkers; the Zimbabwe African National Union, which was leading Rhodesia's armed Black liberation struggle; and Oakland Concerned Citizens for Urban Renewal. Elaine consulted frequently with David about the newspaper's coverage of the party's work with these groups.

The paper frequently reprinted articles from other leftist and progressive publications whose views reflected those of the BPP. Writers were given news clippings to edit. Such reprints were always attributed in an editor's note. Unlike most other leftist publications, however, there were no bylines on articles in the *Black Panther*.

Ideas and some copy for national and international news often came from establishment newspapers like the *New York Times*, *Los Angeles Times*, and *Washington Post*. However, our slant on the major news events of the day was almost always different than what appeared in the establishment papers. Under David's brilliant leadership, the quality, language, and appearance of the *Black Panther* substantially improved. The party purchased a good-quality offset typesetting machine and made greater use of party members with writing skills for proofreading and copyediting.

Membership Drops: *Black Panther* Becomes Biweekly

Police surveillance of the newspaper continued. According to a Los Angeles Police Department intelligence division memo of March 11, 1974, "*The Black Panther* has increased in journalistic quality but decreased in circulation since the Panthers have concentrated in the Oakland area."

David's tenure as editor ended abruptly in early 1976 when his mother, Shirley Graham Du Bois, widow of Dr. W. E. B. Du Bois, became ill and David left Oakland to care for her in Beijing, China, where she died in 1977. Of his work with the BPP, David later said, "It irrevocably, mercifully changed my life." After his mother's death, David divided much of his time between living in Cairo, Egypt, and Amherst, Massachusetts, where for many years he was a visiting professor of Afro-American studies and journalism at the University of Massachusetts. When he was in the United States, David and I would often talk by phone about the pressing issues of the day. In September 1999, I invited him to attend a meeting of Black activists that I helped to organize in Atlanta. David's contributions to the meeting were invaluable and deeply appreciated by the mostly young people who attended. David died on January 28, 2005, in Amherst after a short illness. He was seventy-nine.

Following David as editor was Michael Fultz, the talented assistant editor, a Brooklyn native who joined the party in Boston while a college student. Michael became editor of the *Black Panther* when the BPP was mounting a citywide campaign to elect Lionel Wilson as Oakland's first Black mayor. Elaine told party members that Wilson's election was an essential condition for creating a favorable climate for Huey's return from Cuba to stand trial on the assault and murder charges from August 1974. As the party's official news organ, the newspaper was a key component in the Wilson campaign and efforts to bring Huey home. Elaine, therefore, often instructed Michael on the paper's contents. In addition to his responsibilities as editor, Michael often spoke for the party at meetings and other community events.

In April 1977, Wilson was elected mayor of Oakland, and Huey returned to Oakland from Cuba in July. He was later acquitted of assaulting Preston Callins but stood trial twice for the murder of Kathleen Smith. Both trials ended in mistrials, and charges were dropped in 1979. As a result of Huey's three costly trials and several unrelated arrests, party resources were nearly depleted, and membership further declined. Soon after I became editor of the newspaper in March 1978, following Michael's resignation from the party, problems developed in my marriage to Joe Abron. He was among several Panthers who left the party in the late 1970s, and we later were divorced. BPP membership, variously estimated at highs of two thousand to four thousand nationwide, had dropped to only a couple of dozen. Most members, although still dedicated to the party's principles, found it hard to stay in the organization as they got older and found themselves needing and wanting better living conditions for themselves and their families, which the party could not provide. The newspaper cadre had only six members, down from thirteen in 1974. With fewer people to produce the newspaper, the *Black Panther* became a biweekly.

Tragedy in Jonestown

The reduction in the newspaper's staff and frequency did not soften its stance on issues affecting Black and poor people. One example was the *Black Panther*'s account of the November 1978 deaths of over nine hundred Americans, mostly Black and many children, in Jonestown, a settlement in the Caribbean nation of Guyana.

The Jonestown dead were members of the San Francisco–based Peoples Temple, a church founded by the Reverend Jim Jones. The BPP had developed a close relationship with Peoples Temple, whose community programs for the poor in San Francisco and Northern California were much like those of the party. I knew a few Temple members and considered them my comrades in the struggle. Charles Garry, longtime BPP attorney, was also attorney for Peoples Temple.

Stanley Nelson, director of the 2006 documentary *Jonestown: The Life and Death of the Peoples Temple*, said in a newspaper interview that his film attempted to portray the "thin lines between faith and zealotry." After I saw the film, I found myself wondering, where does religious faith end and zealotry begin? At any rate, in 1978, the BPP, based on our ties with the church, believed that Jones and several hundred church members had exiled themselves to Guyana and established Jonestown to protest racism and poverty in the United States. To Black Panthers, Jonestown was a serious indictment of life in America. The settlement could prove to be an embarrassment to the US government if allowed to continue.

California congressman Leo Ryan, several Bay Area journalists, and attorney Charles Garry went to Jonestown in November 1978 to investigate complaints from relatives of Jonestown settlers. Authorities said that Peoples Temple members, afraid that they would be forced to disband Jonestown, committed suicide by drinking poisoned Flavor Aid at Jones's direction. Jones was found shot to death, apparently having committed suicide. Ryan and three journalists with him were killed while boarding their plane to fly back to the United States.

The BPP questioned whether the mass deaths were really suicide. In the beginning, we had no concrete evidence to support our suspicions. However, the strident media campaign to discredit Jones and Peoples Temple as a "crazy cult" in the weeks following the tragedy reminded many Panthers of the FBI COINTELPRO campaign against the party. Some party members, including me, were convinced that the deaths at Jonestown might also be the result of COINTELPRO actions.

To substantiate our beliefs, *Black Panther* writers interviewed members of Peoples Temple and their relatives; we read dozens of news articles about the church. I went several days without sleep to gather the story on Jonestown. For me, it became a personal crusade to tell the truth about how the Peoples Temple members died.

Six weeks in the making, an entire issue of the *Black Panther* was devoted to what we called the Jonestown "massacre." I wrote the banner headline on the front page of the paper: "CIA Linked to Deaths in Jonestown." I also wrote many of the articles in the issue. One of those, quoting other news sources, charged that a top aide to Jones had once been a CIA agent.

In the editorial, which I wrote, the BPP accused the CIA of destroying Jonestown with a neutron bomb, which is colorless and odorless and doesn't leave any evidence. This was a bold charge, even for the BPP, and I knew it had to be approved by Huey prior to publication.

In all my phone conversations with him, never had I been as nervous as I was that January day in 1979 when I read the editorial on Jonestown. Despite the public damage to Huey's image from the assault and murder trials he went through after his return from Cuba, he had resumed leadership of the party, and I respected him. After I finished reading him the editorial, he said to my great relief, "Good. Print it."

Many people thought the BPP's assessment of what happened at Jonestown was crazy. One woman said if she believed the BPP's account, she would have to start questioning everything the US government did. She said she was afraid to do that.

Among the websites dedicated to research and information about Jonestown is one created in 1999 by the Department of Religious Studies at San Diego State University. According to this source, documents about Jonestown that were eligible for mandatory declassification on December 31, 2006, were not declassified. Why not?

It has been over thirty years since the horrific deaths at Jonestown, and I no longer believe that it was destroyed by a neutron bomb. However, until all the government documents about Jonestown are released, I believe the truth will never be known about the extent to which the US government was involved in the destruction of Jonestown. Nevertheless, the *Black Panther*'s coverage of the event was but one example of the newspaper's boldness and in-depth reporting of news involving and impacting Black and other disenfranchised people. Even though the programs of the BPP and its membership were decimated by the late seventies, and the *Black Panther* was forced to go monthly in 1980, the paper was still in demand by readers who wanted a nonmainstream analysis of the news.

The Last *Black Panther*, the First *Commemorator*

It was with great sorrow that after thirteen years the BPP was forced to discontinue the paper in October 1980. Much as I loved the paper, I was among those party members who persuaded Huey that we no longer had the human or financial resources to publish "the people's paper."

Over a decade later, in November 1990, the Commemoration Committee for the Black Panther Party—composed of ex-Panthers and BPP supporters—began publication of the *Commemorator* in Oakland. The newspaper's statement of purpose reflected the original goals of the BPP and the *Black Panther*: "The newspaper encourages grassroots organizing and networking for people empowerment and community control of the institutions effecting change . . . the *Commemorator* is a progressive community forum. It offers the community at large the opportunity to help solve some of the critical problems that affect us all . . . the lack of decent shelter, medical care, education, and employment for all people."

Beginning in the November 1990 issue and concluding in the March 1991 issue, the *Commemorator* reprinted an article written in May 1990 by ex-BPP chair Elaine Brown, "Responding to Radical Racism: David Horowitz Barely Remembered." Horowitz, former editor of *Ramparts* magazine, a leftist publication, was once a BPP ally. Elaine's article was written in response to a particularly bitter and racist article by Horowitz in the March–April 1990 issue of *Smart* magazine, in which the white ex-radical accused the BPP of being a "gang of hoodlums" and Huey of being a "thug who had terrorized the Oakland underworld in the seventies." In a stinging rebuke to Horowitz's reactionary charges, Elaine wrote, "That Horowitz chooses to dismiss the holocaustal horror of the Black experience in America in his denunciation of Huey as a 'crazy nigger' serves as clear and convincing evidence of his [Horowitz's] racism." Calling Horowitz a "racist white rabbit" who was trying to confuse all who entered "his wonderland," Elaine then accused him of using Huey to discredit the progressive movement. "Depicting the support of the campaign to 'Free Huey!' by Whites and non-Panthers as the development of 'a cult,' Horowitz clucks a reprobate tongue at the serious work of literally millions of people. . . . There was no 'cult,' but a coalition by a mass of people consciously addressing yearnings and demands that came to focus on the freedom of one man, as he personified the capture of a collective freedom."

The April 1991 issue of the *Commemorator* included an excerpt from Huey's doctoral dissertation, "War against the Panthers." In the December 1, 2005, issue of the *Commemorator*, former Black Panther Melvin Dickson, the *Commemorator* editor, wrote a tribute to the late Rosa Parks.

Memorial Issue of the *Black Panther*

Following on the heels of the *Commemorator*, in February 1991, in Berkeley the Black Panther Newspaper Committee (BPNC), a nonprofit organization of former Panthers, published a memorial issue of the *Black Panther* that looked like a *Black Panther* issue of the late 1960s. Using the newspaper's original masthead from the sixties, the front page of the paper featured the famous 1967 photo of Huey and

Bobby dressed in the BPP uniform of black leather jackets and black berets, standing in front of party headquarters with guns, and the banner headline "The Struggle Continues." The editorial said in part: "We were all members of the Black Panther Party who participated in the formation, organization, and day-to-day operations of Black Panther Party activities. . . . Because of our uncompromising work to build a strong Afrikan-Amerikkkan nation . . . many of us were forced into exile or underground or were imprisoned by the US government during its COINTELPRO war."

The editorial said that the memorial issue came together out of a "compelling need" to address such critical issues in the African American community as drugs, unemployment, inadequate housing, miseducation, "legalized police terror and murder," and institutional racism—issues addressed in the BPP Ten-Point Platform and Program. The editorial concluded, "In the past *The Black Panther Black Community News Service* was an uncompromising voice for exposing these attacks . . . and for advocating an implacable stand to redress them. . . . We are proud to announce to you that uncompromising voice has returned!"

The memorial issue was dedicated to the BPP's fallen comrades, party members killed by police or other law enforcement agents and those held as political prisoners. The issue contained photos and biographies of some of the fallen comrades and articles about the cases of several political prisoners. Other articles were written by some of those prisoners, several of whom were BPP members. Also included in the memorial issue were the Ten-Point Platform and Program, a chronology of party history from 1966 to 1971, a description and photos of the party's survival programs, articles on then-current national and international news, and a financial statement about the expenses and income of the memorial issue.

Renewed Interest in the BPP

Spurred by the autobiographies and memoirs of such former Panther leaders as Elaine Brown, Kathleen Cleaver, and David Hilliard, as well as the 1995 film *Panther*, there was a nationwide resurgence of interest in the BPP. This renewed interest by Black youth, activists, and scholars contributed to the creation of new Black Panther groups around the country beginning in the early 1990s. Those groups included the Black Panther Militia, founded by former BPP member and former Milwaukee City Council member Michael McGee; the New Black Panther Party for Self-Defense, created in Dallas by Aaron Michaels, which nationally grew under the leadership of the late Dr. Khalid Muhammad, previously the national spokesman for the Nation of Islam; and the New Panther Vanguard Movement in Los Angeles, established by Kwaku Duren, who in the late 1970s was appointed by Elaine Brown to coordinate the revived Southern California BPP chapter.

Unfortunately, some of these new Panther formations did not learn from the mistakes of the original Black Panther Party. Sectarianism, factional disputes, and personality cults that developed around various leaders prevented the new Panther groups from uniting under one umbrella. At the thirty-fifth reunion of the Black Panther Party, held in 2002 in Washington, DC, Ron Scott, cofounder of the original Detroit chapter of the BPP, and I led a workshop on the new Panther movements. Some members of the New Black

Panther Party for Self-Defense attended the workshop, and Ron and I criticized them for misrepresenting the history of the original BPP on the New Black Panther Party website by replacing Bobby Seale's picture with that of Khalid Muhammad in a famous photo of Huey and Bobby. The doctored photo was subsequently removed from the New BPP website.

The New BPP periodically published the *Black Panther Black Community News Service*. The New Panther Vanguard Movement revived the *Black Panther Intercommunal News Service* and published new issues from 1997 to 2001. Several issues of the original Black Panther newspaper may be found on the website of It's About Time, www.itsabouttimeBPP.com. It's About Time, a network of Panther alumni and supporters to which I belong, organized thirtieth, thirty-fifth, fortieth, and fiftieth anniversary Panther reunions. (With former BPP members Madalynn C. Rucker and the late Ralph Moore, I organized the twentieth-anniversary reunion held in Oakland, in October 1986.) It's About Time is based in Sacramento and coordinated by former BPP member William "Billy X" Jennings. To preserve Huey's legacy, Huey's widow, Frederika Newton, and David Hilliard, former BPP chief of staff, founded the Dr. Huey P. Newton Foundation in 1994, which can be found at www.hueypnewtonfoundation.org.

In 1998, *The Black Panther Party [Reconsidered]* was published by Black Classic Press, whose founder, W. Paul Coates, is a former BPP member. Edited by Dr. Charles E. Jones, founding chair of the Department of African American Studies at Georgia State University, *The Black Panther Party [Reconsidered]* is perhaps the most comprehensive anthology of essays and memoirs written to date about the original BPP. (My essay "Serving the People: The Survival Programs of the Black Panther Party," now chapter 6 of this volume, was first published in it.)

Enduring Contributions of the BPP

In October 2006 I joined many of my former Panther comrades and friends and supporters at the BPP's fortieth anniversary celebration in Oakland. As I rejoiced at seeing old friends, I was reminded that the struggle of African Americans for justice and equality, outlined in the party's Ten-Point Platform and Program of October 15, 1966, continues. There is still no "land, bread, housing, education, clothing, justice and peace" for a vast majority of Black people in America.

The Black Panther Party founded by Huey P. Newton and Bobby Seale arose from the unique economic, social, and political conditions that existed among Black people in the United States in the late twentieth century. Those conditions cannot be re-created. Consequently, the Black Panther Party cannot be re-created. However, the various attempts to do so underscore the enduring contributions of the BPP to the empowerment of Black and disenfranchised people throughout the world.

CHAPTER 4

Fulfilling the Mission

Each generation must out of relative obscurity discover its mission, fulfill it, or betray it.
—Frantz Fanon, The Wretched of the Earth

By the fall of 1963, CORE activist Hardy Frye had moved from Los Angeles to Sacramento following the breakup of his first marriage. He worked for a time as a clerk for the Greyhound bus company and was active in demonstrations and other activities of the local CORE chapter. He was laid off at Greyhound and was at the unemployment office to get a check on November 22, 1963, when the announcement was made that President John F. Kennedy had been assassinated. When the unemployment office attempted to shut down, Hardy said he protested.

"I was in there saying . . . 'You better get me a check or I ain't going. I don't have any way to pay my rent'. . . . There was a white guy standing right behind me . . . and he started screaming too, and so we started screaming [that] we would refuse to leave. We were raising so much hell that they took us to the state director of unemployment. He drew out the checks that day. . . . That was the first time that I had ever had to, as an individual, confront the system by myself in that kind of fashion," Hardy said.

While on a CORE picket line protesting the small number of Black employees at a bottling plant, Hardy said he met a college professor who would be "very instrumental" in his life. "This guy was brilliant. I began to discuss a lot of my ideas about Marxism [with him]. We spent many days sitting around discussing the French Revolution and race revolution because [the professor] was an historian. So that was very important in my life in terms of my getting into the . . . historical context of the politics I had been moving close to . . . and why I should go to school." Hardy later entered the graduate program in sociology at the University of California, Berkeley, where at the time he was the only Black teaching assistant. "I won an award for best student. They told me they were giving it to a Negro because it was time for a Negro to win," Hardy said.

He joined a Friends of SNCC committee that was formed in Sacramento. In the summer of 1964, Hardy, then twenty-five, volunteered to work on SNCC voter registration drives and other SNCC projects in Mississippi. "What was so great about it was that we practiced participatory democracy, which, when I think about it, must have been crazy," Hardy said. But it was a fantastic experience where you really got up and said what you felt, and people took you seriously." In the summer of 1966, he led a SNCC voting rights march in Tennessee.

Traveling back and forth from Sacramento to Mississippi until early 1968, Hardy combined his college studies with community organizing in the Black Sacramento neighborhood of Oak Park. There his work brought him into contact with the Black Panther Party. When several Black Panthers were arrested after they marched into the California state legislature on May 2, 1967, some Oak Park activists helped to bail the Panthers out of jail. Hardy subsequently became the SNCC representative in Sacramento.

When SNCC national chairman Stokely Carmichael gave his "Black Power" speech in Mississippi in June 1966, most SNCC workers viewed it favorably. Hardy said that he did not:

> I was totally freaked out because it was nationalistic to me. Through the early sixties, in the sit-ins around the [California] state capitol, most of my allies were white. Most of the people who were in CORE were white. I went down to Mississippi, and there were more white people in the 1964 summer project than there were Black people. I know you don't turn your back on someone who's been your ally just because he's white, who's been in jail with you, who's gone through all this stuff. At some point, I saw us all as being guerrillas in war. . . . So, you don't see color in the sense that I would later come to see it in terms of the movement. I didn't understand this strong nationalist swing all of a sudden.

In Dallas, the mother of the leader of the city's SNCC chapter was inspired by her son's activism in the Black liberation struggle. Known as "Mama Mac" by her friends, Eva Partee McMillan was born in 1921 in Bradford, Tennessee, the youngest (along with her twin sister) of eight children of a farmer and a housekeeper. The family later moved to Dallas, where Mama Mac completed high school and married Ernest McMillan Sr., a Methodist minister, with whom she had four children.

"I didn't become organized until SNCC formed its chapter," Mama Mac said. "My son [Ernest "Ernie" McMillan Jr.] was a student at Morehouse College in Atlanta and dropped out to join SNCC. He worked with it in Alabama, Georgia, and Mississippi for two or three years and then came back to Dallas to open a SNCC chapter here. The news media came out and interviewed my son and got all this information about Black Power. In Dallas, people didn't know what it was or what it meant."

SNCC and its national chairman at the time, Stokely Carmichael, were among the initial Black organizations and leaders targeted in 1967 by the FBI's counterintelligence program to "disrupt and destroy," according to a 1976 report by the US Senate Intelligence Committee. Soon after the Dallas SNCC chapter opened in 1967, the police began to harass her son Ernie, Mama Mac said. She recalled, "Two or three police cars would be parked in front of my house all the time. I didn't have to worry about robbers or anything because I had the police there. Each time my son would come out of the house, they would arrest him. If he'd pull off in a car and go half a block just shifting his gears, they would charge him with speeding. He quit driving. He started walking. [Then] they'd stop him and say, 'Let's see, McMillan. Maybe we'll charge you with jaywalking this time.'"

In 1968, a few months after the assassination of Martin Luther King Jr., the Dallas SNCC chapter organized a boycott of a white-owned supermarket chain that had several stores in the city's mostly poor Black neighborhoods, Mama Mac said. SNCC accused the chain of discriminatory hiring practices and of selling overpriced and low-quality products.

"I stopped in one of the stores and got some eggs," Mama Mac explained. "I got home and cracked one, and it was rotten. I cracked all twelve, and they were all rotten. That's what the neighbors were incensed about, and they called SNCC and asked would they help them picket the store. So, they did." Ernie McMillan was arrested for destroying several items in one of the stores. (Sentenced to ten years in prison, he fled the country.) Angered at the persecution of her son, Mama Mac herself became active in Black Power politics in Dallas.

In Brooklyn, New York, the movement for community-controlled schools helped to replace the hopelessness that had "controlled" the Black community, according to Rev. C. Herbert Oliver. "We wanted our children to get an education that would help them cope with life, and we knew they were not getting it," Oliver said, adding that things changed after the creation of the Ocean Hill–Brownsville (OHB) school board in 1967. "There was a hope that something good would happen now." At times, Oliver, president of the board, said that he presided over meetings that were attended by five hundred or six hundred people. Prior to that, only a handful of people would attend PTA meetings.

The OHB experimental school district board was made up of seven parents, five community representatives, and supposedly seven teachers and two school administrators, Oliver said. "This arrangement gave the voting edge to the community," which was important because most of the white teachers opposed the board, Oliver said. He and a "nonconformist" Catholic priest, "a fighter who was always attacking the system," coordinated the election of the teacher representatives to the board. Recalling how the election process worked, Rev. Oliver said that he and the priest went around to each of the seven schools in the district. "Each school we entered, the teachers greeted us like we were lions or something. We were [considered] dangerous people. . . . After a few weeks, Rhody McCoy, the OHB administrator, put an order out to the schools that those who were interested should gather after school and elect teacher representatives. Most of the Black teachers came and elected Black representatives to the board. The white teachers stayed away and would not participate."

One of the first tasks of the board was to secure mentors, usually adult Black men, for "incorrigible" students, Oliver said.

> We wanted to bring in people in the community and have them work with the young people, people that you might see one day shopping in the grocery store, in church. Somebody that you don't lose after school closes after three o'clock. That was the position we had when we began. If you don't have contact with the community, you don't have contact with the children, and discipline becomes a problem. The men would bring the students to school and make them function. White teachers weren't able to do that because they had no connection with people in the community. They came into the community [to teach] and then went back home, which was miles away.

To further improve the atmosphere in the classrooms, McCoy hired "parent professionals" to work as teachers' aides, and many unemployed people were able to work and to also learn what was going on in the schools. According to Oliver, the board used its decision-making powers over curriculum to institute the Montessori teaching method. A major complaint of Black parents in the OHB district was the lack of Black principals in the public schools. At the time, some eight hundred people were on the eligibility list to be a principal, and at that rate "it would have taken forty to fifty years for Blacks to get in," Oliver said. Largely through the efforts of McCoy, a Black person who was qualified to be a principal but was not on the waiting list was hired. One Black principal kept his position for over twenty years and "did an excellent job working with the young people and leading them in a new direction," Oliver said. "Many of those young people went on to college." Oliver said that the first Puerto Rican and first Chinese principals in New York City public schools were hired during this time.

A major ally of the OHB board and the movement for community-controlled schools was the Brooklyn chapter of CORE, then led by Sonny Carson (Mwlina Imiri Abubadika). During the New York City teachers' strike in the fall of 1968, the OHB board was under attack by the teachers' union, Rev. Oliver said. "There came a time when there was some expectation [that] something [might] be done to our board." At one board meeting, he said:

> Sonny Carson stationed his young men all around the school [where the meeting was held]. They were ready for a shootout. They perceived themselves as protecting our board. Hundreds of policemen were all around the school. But they didn't bother with Carson's men. I think they knew if they had, there would have been a lot of bloodshed. [Carson's men] were the militants. They were ready to fight and die. We [OHB board] were not violent. We did not ask for that kind of support, but

> they offered it. When we told them we didn't need it, we could tell them without breaking with them. Everything was cool. We were OK.

The teachers' union in New York City, which "fought [the OHB board] on every score," Oliver said, eventually succeeded in weakening the city's movement for community-controlled schools.

The Brooklyn chapter of the National Welfare Rights Organization was very supportive of the OHB movement for community-controlled schools, said Jackie Pope, who was an NWRO activist. "It was mainly people who were on welfare who were involved" in the OHB movement, she said. "We worked with them on the picket lines. We kept our kids out of school during the teachers' strike. (Jackie's daughters went to a Catholic school.) We put the kids back in school when these young Jewish professionals came in there to teach. They were wonderful. They said reading levels gained three and four years [during the strike]."

The Brooklyn chapter became one of the NWRO's largest chapters in the United States. At her first meeting, Jackie said, she was "scared and appalled" by what she learned about the US welfare system. "They were talking about a system that I firmly believed was there to help me. I didn't want to rock the boat in any way, because I [thought] I would be homeless," she said.

Despite her initial misgivings about the welfare rights movement, Jackie got involved. "At one point the welfare rights movement actually ran classes, and the classes were taught by people on public assistance," she said. "People on public assistance would come to the welfare rights meetings, classes, and training sessions that we had. . . . We had it all together. People came to these sessions in droves, and they came because they felt comfortable. You could bring your babies. People who were talking to you were getting the same type of check you were getting every month. No one felt uncomfortable. When we went down to the welfare department, we represented other welfare clients in getting what they were entitled to. Our model was [that] the welfare rights person who is our member was always right. Even if she was wrong, she was right. You had to get her later and say, 'You know you lied. What is wrong with you?' In front of people, they were right."

Brooklyn's NWRO educated its mostly poor, Black, female members about the rights of welfare recipients. "[We were] outraged at the deprivation that we lived through," Jackie said. She explained: "We got a group of women together to go down to the department of social services and demand to get what we were entitled to . . . we discovered that we were entitled to two sheets, two blankets, underwear, forks and spoons, boots, and raincoats. We were never revolutionary. We always just wanted to be part of America and be like everyone else. We didn't want the stigma of being treated differently."

The Brooklyn welfare rights movement also exposed the racist treatment of women of color who received public assistance, Jackie said.

> We found out that there were almost two separate systems [of treatment]. The people that lived in the cities, mainly people of color, got one treatment, whereas people who lived in the suburbs, mainly European Americans, were given all those basics that [people of color] had to fight for. We found out that once you

> apply for public assistance, you are to be brought up to standards and given grants that would keep you at the level that you were used to living, which was scrupulously followed for suburban women, so that if their husbands deserted them and they were in a house, they got their mortgages paid. In the city, there was a whole different ball game. You couldn't have an extra pair of shoes. A television set and a phone were [considered] luxury items. A phone is not a luxury item! We demonstrated in order to have a right to a phone.

Through a series of campaigns, Jackie said, the Brooklyn NWRO also succeeded in getting policies established that required utility companies to give sufficient notification before cutting off customers' service for lack of payment and for getting proper treatment from the bank that issued checks for welfare recipients. "[Bank officials] treated us like slime and scum," Jackie said. "They had one window where we could go cash our checks. There were even times when we had to stand outside in the back of the bank. We would pray that people coming by who knew we were cashing our checks would not mug us."

Jackie subsequently became the spokeswoman for the Brooklyn chapter of the NWRO. "It was my job to make sure I got to the press by any means necessary," she said. In the late 1960s she was a national training coordinator for the NWRO, worked at the group's headquarters in Washington, DC, and was the editor of the NWRO newspaper.

In 1969 Joyce Grant was hired as the first principal of the New School for Children in Boston. Like the elementary schools in Brooklyn's experimental school district, the New School was one of the first community-run public schools in the country. The school's board of directors included well-known author Jonathan Kozol, Joyce said. "New School was conceived, initiated, and operated by Black parents. They were fantastic. It was a wonderful experience. I learned what the parents learned. I learned on the job how to run a school, how to think about education. [Community-run schools] were good schools that in a sense proved Black kids could learn. They just needed someone to teach them."

New School was housed in one of several buildings left vacant by the Catholic Church in Roxbury, a predominantly African American community in Boston. The school was supported by private and foundation grants. As principal, Joyce had a major role in fundraising for the school. "I was always going out and getting the money. I would put my blue suit on and go out to Cambridge [a white, suburban community] and talk about schools and the needs of Black kids," she said. Joyce was later hired as one of the first African American faculty members in the School of Education at Northeastern University, she said. Located in Roxbury, Northeastern then had some thirty-five thousand students but fewer than twenty Black faculty members. Her hiring caused "much resentment," Joyce said, because at the time she did not have a doctoral degree, which is usually required of college faculty. Nevertheless, she said that she set out to correct what she believed was a major problem at the School of Education: it did not place its graduates in Boston public schools, where a large number of students were minorities.

"I was quite upset about that and was told I could find teaching positions for ten graduates but that I was 'going to be responsible' for them, like someone was going to [otherwise] kill them or something," Joyce said. With support from Northeastern's dean of education (who was "a raving liberal," according to Joyce), she helped to raise awareness among the faculty about the importance of cultural diversity in education.

Elsewhere on the East Coast in the late 1960s, Zakiya Somburu helped to start a Black Student Union (BSU) at the predominantly Black East Orange High School in New Jersey. "[Black students at the school] wanted to be able to be more expressive in our blackness, and we felt that those issues were not being addressed," Zakiya told me. "I remember one instructor in particular, in history, who challenged us to have a debate, because this was when there was the issue of ethnic studies at Rutgers University." Some Black students subsequently took over a building during a protest demanding the creation of an ethnic studies program at the state university. In May 1969, Rutgers officials came to East Orange High to recruit Black students, Zakiya said. "I'll never forget that. We never saw them [Rutgers recruiters] before then, but they came out to try to get representation of Black folks . . . after their building was seized." Zakiya said the BSU at East Orange High wasn't as political as it should have been. "We were very interested in [Black] culture, so we had fashion shows, and we did the African garb and that kind of stuff. We were more or less culturally oriented." The BSU also organized study groups. Zakiya recalled: "It was in vogue to read . . . books on Black history, on the Black movement. If you weren't doing that you were really kind of on the outs." As a teenager, she insisted that her boyfriends be knowledgeable about the Black liberation struggle. "I didn't want to be bothered with dummies."

After graduating from high school in June 1969, Zakiya moved to Los Angeles. There, in 1970, at age eighteen, she had her first child, a son, and got married. After she gave birth at a county hospital, she was in a ward with nine or ten other women. "I saw social workers come around with papers, coercing these young women to sign to get sterilized. There was one woman next to me who was very distraught. . . . For whatever reason, the father of the child was not around, and she felt very alienated, isolated. She signed the papers. I pleaded with her not to do that. I was very young at the time, but I knew that she was just signing away her reproductive rights to the state. That experience really stayed with me when I got involved in reproductive rights."

In 1972 Zakiya moved with her husband and son to Oakland. Not long afterward, her marriage ended, and she took two jobs "trying to survive" and raise her son. She became "very disillusioned with society, the way it was set up," she said. "There were a few Black people that were the upper class . . . that had money . . . but the vast majority of Black folk were in desperate poverty. I started looking at the societal arrangement [and thinking] there is something wrong with this. I saw the disparities that existed, and I felt that I needed to become increasingly involved in political activity."

Zakiya started reading a lot "to broaden my theoretical base of understanding." And she was angry: "I was pissed off, and I had to use that energy to get politically involved because I felt very explosive. That is how I can really understand how rebellions take place and people just have had it." In 1974, near the end of the Black Power era, Zakiya joined the Socialist Workers Party (SWP). After "drilling" some members of the SWP, particularly Black members, Zakiya said she chose the group because of its "political clarity" and consistency working in the Black community.

Zakiya added, "In order to be an effective socialist, you have to be a Black nationalist first. I saw no contradiction being a nationalist and a socialist, and I was definitely a feminist." She said that the Black Power movement did not sufficiently address issues involving Black women. "I saw a lot of chauvinistic attitudes practiced by brothers [in Black Power groups]." She recalled one incident involving a female high school classmate of hers who joined a Black Power group and said she was going to have children "for the revolution." Zakiya said to her, "You are too young to do that. What are you going to do with your life?" And she told me: "There [was] a lot of baggage . . . insofar as the issue of oppression of women . . . that I just could not buy into."

At the Black Topographical Research Center in Kalamazoo, Michigan, Black women were excluded from leadership, said Joye Williams, whose first husband was a member of "the Top." "The women were not privy to a lot of details of the organization. . . . My understanding was that there were [Top] branches in Kalamazoo, New Jersey, Los Angeles, and Chicago."

On the walls of the organization's office, Joye said, information was posted "in the form of charts, graphs, and pictures."

> The idea was to give a tour to share information about Black people's condition in the US. The men (many who were students at Western Michigan University) gave the tour. . . . There were maps that had been carefully drawn and had been color-coded. They showed where Black people lived. They talked about ownership of land, manufacturing. . . . At the end of the tour, they [said] that someday there would be a

> Black revolution. . . . [The tour] was actually like a lecture, where the brothers would stand with pointers and move from chart to chart. You would follow them visually as they moved around the room. It was kind of like a classroom.

The Top in Kalamazoo didn't sponsor events in the community and didn't work with other groups, Joye said. "The Top focused on its goals, which I thought were admirable . . . to teach about the conditions that were affecting Blacks." Male members were given the title of "commander." "You could be a commander one or a . . . ten, with one being the highest. The men did the teaching and the recruiting. The women did none of this kind of thing. It was clearly defined by the men what everyone's role was going to be," Joye said.

The Black Law Society was a spin-off group from the Top. According to Joye, "There was a list of Black laws (codes) that said how men and women should be, how everything should be." Joye said she was unsure of the origin of the codes but that it was "mostly instructional, how you should conduct yourself . . . [and] how you should deal with your family."

At the Champaign-Urbana campus of the University of Illinois, one of the first tasks that faced Tony Zamora after he became the director of the Black Cultural Center in 1970 was winning the trust and support of the Black students. He did not plan it this way, Tony said, but he earned the students' support when he briefly resigned shortly after taking over as the center's director. The incident that prompted his resignation, he said, occurred when the head of the campus Afro-American Commission would not accept the budget for the center that he had asked Tony to prepare.

The day after he resigned, Tony said, "Three hundred students were in the office [of the head of the Afro-American Commission]. Then he resigned, and [the administration] asked me to come back. From that moment on, I began to feel the value of students in terms of their support. It also gave a message to the university that if you have somebody there that the students felt as though they could trust, then something could be done." To give the center more visibility, Tony said he used his previous experience working for a publishing house to produce a brochure about the center.

Tony already had credibility in the local Black community, in which he had been politically active for several years prior to becoming director of the center, he said. "I brought in a lot of good things that hadn't been seen before on that campus (such as jazz singer Nina Simone), and I've got the letters today to demonstrate that. That was one of the things that really started me really understanding what the center was about." However, after a year on the job, student demands on him became too much, Tony said. "I was putting in fifteen hours a day, from one night to the next. I was plainly overwhelmed. After time, it wasn't in my best interest to work under these conditions, and I stepped out of it."

After a year of rest and reflection, Tony was hired in 1972 as director of the Black Cultural Center at Purdue University in West Lafayette, Indiana. The center had opened in 1970 as part of the university's Black Student Programs, and Tony was the center's first full-time director. He was also an assistant director of Purdue's student union. "The general consensus was that I wouldn't last six months because I had this dual responsibility. The university was really trying to bring Blacks into the student union board. I had to wear two hats." Tony added that he developed a good working rapport with the student union's director. "He realized that if I could look good, I could make him look good. It was upward mobility for him."

Once on the job, he said, he found that Purdue's Black Cultural Center lacked a sense of direction. "There was no programmatic focus that was stable. I wasn't totally sure what would work at Purdue. It was a different environment than the University of Illinois, a much more conservative campus. The University of Illinois had a large influence of students from Chicago, [which gave it] a different cultural mindset. Purdue is in what I call the gospel belt."

In time, Tony assembled a full-time staff and created ongoing programs at the center. "People rallied to my cause, saw what was needed, and came in and helped me," he said. "What I wanted to do was to surround the center with people who were capable and knowledgeable . . . a collective of people who had objectives. I began to use the center as a mecca for employing [Black] students. There were leadership workshops and training by professionals in developing good work habits. I . . . used the staff meetings with students to talk about issues related to the Black condition." The center's library was a "gold mine," Tony said. During his twenty-two-year tenure at the center, he acquired an extensive collection of Afrocentric books and other materials for the center's library and hired a full-time librarian.

In Detroit, in the aftermath of the Black community's rebellion in July 1967, the *Inner City Voice*, the newspaper created by Mike Hamlin and John Watson, flourished, Mike said.

> It was our contention that we had to write in the language of the people we were trying to mobilize. So, the

> language that we used was quite earthy, brutally frank, and didn't mince any words. We cursed; we labeled people. It was very powerful language. . . . It was successful, but we couldn't keep a steady printer because after the first edition, the white printers wouldn't print it. We went from one printer to the next. We finally wound up with a printer who was in the Communist Party. The paper was a success. It attracted all kinds of Black people.

Black autoworkers in Detroit who were confronted with racism at the plants where they worked were among those attracted to the *Inner City Voice*. One of them was General Baker, "the most respected and significant brother in political struggle in the Detroit area," Mike said. Baker had been fired from the Dodge Main plant, where Mike and his comrades decided to publish a newsletter. "We came up with the name Dodge Revolutionary Union Movement, DRUM. . . . Those publications were a hit. We gave them out free at the [plant's] gate. This was a huge plant. We built a tremendous following," Mike said. The anticommunist sentiment created by Senator Joe McCarthy in the 1950s had caused leftists and radicals to stop distributing literature at the Dodge Main plant. However, Mike said, "We openly and boldly went to the gate and passed the newsletter out. We had sufficient forces and sufficient anger that we were prepared to knock down anybody who tried to stop us, police . . . or otherwise." To prevent the workers at the plant from being fired for distributing the DRUM newsletter, people who didn't work at the plant passed the newsletter out.

The DRUM movement grew, organizing workers around

conditions in the plant. At Sunday meetings, Mike said, workers would tell stories about what happened to them while on the job. “I chaired the meetings mostly because we knew [the plant] had spies,” Mike said. He and Baker wrote “incendiary and inflammatory” articles for the newsletter about the workers’ stories. According to Mike, “We were intimidating to the white workers, but we didn’t care.” He also said that DRUM attracted an increasing number of supporters among students, intellectuals, and middle-class people.

Ultimately, people associated with the DRUM and the *Inner City Voice* formed the League of Revolutionary Black Workers. Mike explained how the league started: “We had a bookstore, a coffee shop, and even got into filmmaking. We needed a forum to incorporate them all. We decided we would establish the League of Revolutionary Black Workers. We were involved in community organizing, decentralization of schools, et cetera. The league could mobilize all these constituencies around particular events. I took on the responsibility of organizing white leftists in the city, who were in total disarray and disorganization. We were able to facilitate that and to bring together some people and cause them to unite and to begin to build a strong organization.”

After arriving in Chicago in January 1964 to serve as pastor of Christ Church Woodlawn, Fr. Earl Neil became active in The Woodlawn Organization (TWO), a coalition of South Side community organizations in which several churches were active. “There was a high degree of Black consciousness among all age levels in the African American community,” he said. “There was a strong affirmation of . . . Black is beautiful.” TWO and other community groups focused on education, unemployment, and ending the gang activity on the city's South and West Sides as ways to bring about social change in Chicago's Black communities, Father Neil said.

At the time, Black people were becoming increasingly disenchanted with the unwillingness of local, state, and federal government agencies to enforce existing civil rights laws. Father Neil said, "There was a whole mood of taking a [defensive] posture and not just engaging in nonviolent resistance as the only option." Led by Martin Luther King Jr., the Southern Christian Leadership Conference (SCLC) held several civil rights marches in the Chicago area during the late 1960s, and the Episcopal Church participated in many of the marches, Father Neil said. Some Chicago-area whites were violent toward SCLC marchers, and the police often had to protect the marchers. "Nazi parties and other white groups were openly organized so it was just seething, just a cauldron of violence," Father Neil said. "[By the beginning of 1967], whenever we would go on a march, we would meet at a place and have a mass rally. Then people were assigned to go to different areas of the city wherever we were demonstrating. We were always advised to be nonviolent but to get home the best way you can. That even got the blessing of Dr. King. He said that nonviolence was a way of life for him, but he couldn't dictate that it be a way of life for everybody." In July 1967 Father Neil moved to Oakland to serve as pastor of St. Augustine's Episcopal Church. "Oakland was so much more laid back than my experience in Chicago," he said. "It was difficult for me at first to see what was going on, anything like racism." In October 1967, Black Panther minister of defense Huey P. Newton was arrested for killing a white Oakland police officer and wounding another during a shootout in which Huey was seriously wounded. At the time, Father Neil said, one of the members of his church was Huey's girlfriend, and the St. Augustine's pastor sometimes accompanied his parishioner to Huey's court appearances. Father Neil said that his involvement with the BPP began after he started visiting Huey at the county jail. Eventually the party regularly held political education classes at St. Augustine's.

On April 6, 1968, two days after Dr. King was assassinated, Oakland police shot and killed seventeen-year-old BPP treasurer Bobby Hutton. Father Neil said he suggested that St. Augustine's hold a joint memorial service for King and Bobby Hutton. "A very beautiful, catalytic thing happened after the service," Father Neil said. "Members of the congregation and members of the party just sat around and talked to each other . . . they began to relate to each other as human beings because the party had the stereotypical opinions of handkerchief preachers and all these church people who didn't want to be involved [in the Black struggle], and the members of the congregation had all these wild-eyed [views] about [Black Panthers], black leather jackets and berets and sunglasses, carrying guns. From that point on, it was a turning point in the life of the congregation and perhaps in the perceptions of some of the members of the party." When BPP chairman Bobby Seale announced that the organization wanted to start a free breakfast program for schoolchildren, Father Neil said that he and one of his parishioners began work on setting the program up. Father Neil investigated the necessary building requirements for a breakfast program, he said, and his parishioner consulted with nutritionists about healthy breakfasts for children.

The breakfast program started in January 1969 at Wadsworth Elementary School near St. Augustine's, Father

Neil said. "The first day, we had eleven students, the next day we had twice that number, and the next day we had some thirty. . . . The kids spread the word themselves. . . . Throughout the duration of the program, we were serving on average about 135 meals a day." Along with members of the BPP, members of St. Augustine's and other people in the community procured donations for the breakfast program from grocery stores. Eventually the program moved to St. Augustine's. "When people heard of it, especially the parents, they came and volunteered to cook," Father Neil said. "To this day, I believe they have breakfast programs in schools because of the party's program."

After graduating from high school in 1967 in Grand Rapids, Michigan, Che Parker moved back to his hometown, Battle Creek. There, he met "Spock," a young Black activist and a graduate of Western Michigan University. Che said, "Right after Dr. King was killed, there were ten to fifteen students at Battle Creek Central High School who were kicked out of the school because they had participated in what was considered rioting at the time. They wouldn't let them back in the school. So, we [Spock and Che] started a freedom school."

The two Black men began organizing with other Black activists in southwestern Michigan. "[We] began to align some of our political ideologies with some of the nationalist brothers from Detroit," Che said. "Battle Creek is right between Detroit and Chicago and became kind of a hotbed. We had quite a few people coming from the Lansing/Grand Rapids/Jackson area to our political education classes." He and Spock periodically traveled to Chicago to attend BPP political education classes and asked the party's permission to start a West Michigan Panther chapter. Che said that he and Spock were in Chicago a few days before Fred Hampton, chairman of the Panther chapter in Chicago, and Mark Clark, a Panther from Peoria, Illinois, were assassinated by Chicago police on December 4, 1969. The request for a Southwest Michigan Panther chapter subsequently failed to win approval, Che said. "There were some criteria that I don't think we met in terms of members."

During this time, Che worked a variety of "miscellaneous" jobs. "We were not wanting to work for the slave master anyway. We were doing fairly well but just minimally getting by." Ultimately Che and some other Black male activists decided to set up a West Michigan Council of the Republic of New Afrika. "We set up the provisional government [of the RNA] and elected Richard Henry (Omari Obadele) president for life," Che said. The RNA established its headquarters in Jackson, Mississippi, and purchased several acres of land in a rural area near Biloxi.

One day in August 1971, Che and other members of the West Michigan Council of the RNA had gone to the group's property near Biloxi to help set up facilities, Che said. When they returned to headquarters in Jackson, they learned that local police and FBI agents had raided RNA offices, arresting Omari Obadele and other RNA members on a variety of charges, including trespassing on the rural land they occupied near Biloxi. Che explained, "Some of the paperwork [for the land] had not gone through, and whoever owned the land had not expected to see several hundred Black people on the land." During the raids, a police officer was killed, and another officer and an FBI agent were wounded. Obadele and ten other RNA members were tried for murder; eight were convicted. "It seemed like just as soon as we attempted to do things legally and within the system is where we met our biggest problem," Che said. "I don't think we ever really got a chance to get started."

Nevertheless, he added, the RNA "brought an awful lot of enlightenment in a way that we could express some cultural pride . . . and that was good in the long range. On the short range, I think that only a few individuals got a chance to really catch on and understood what we were trying to do. . . . I think we were right on the verge of solutions."

In the month after Che and other RNA West Michigan Council members returned home from Mississippi, he said he was arrested at least eight times. "We knew for a fact that [police] had all our pictures. . . . We were open targets. We were followed everywhere and harassed quite a bit. A few of us lost jobs, and there were dope setups and things like that."

CHAPTER 5

Struggles and Sacrifices

When you are driven by something and that something demands a lot of you, something is always sacrificed.

—Leoduris (Lee) Rose Weisberg, Black Power era activist

During the Black Power era, some groups tried to work together despite their often very different beliefs and organizing styles. Between 1967 and 1968 the Black Panther Party and the Student Nonviolent Coordinating Committee attempted a merger.

At the time, Hardy Frye was the SNCC representative in Sacramento, and he opposed the merger. According to him, SNCC and the BPP lacked the experience to effectively organize Blacks in America's urban areas. Furthermore, Hardy said that while he often armed himself while working as a SNCC organizer in the "combat zone" of Mississippi, he nevertheless believed that the Panthers' public display of guns during their community patrols of the police was reckless. He also disapproved of an initial BPP policy (that was later changed) that allowed people to walk into a Panther office and immediately sign up for membership.

"Prior to the Black Power thing with SNCC, you earned your stripes by how long you'd spent in jail, for the right kind of issues . . . as well as how well you did in the field. And you slowly got a reputation . . . you just didn't walk into SNCC. . . . We didn't let nobody walk into the organization and run a project." The image of the Panthers that was projected in the media and in the movement was that they were violent, Hardy said. Much later, he said, he learned that there was another "whole set of people in the Panthers whom I never knew" who were not violent. The BPP–SNCC merger ultimately failed, due in part to political differences that could not be overcome and the exploitation of these differences by the FBI's counterintelligence campaign against both groups.

In Detroit, the League of Revolutionary Black Workers had a short-lived alliance with the BPP, according to Mike Hamlin, who was a leader of the league. "We broke with them [the BPP] almost immediately. . . . We were based on the working class, and they were based on the lumpen (a term popularized by Karl Marx referring to a segment of the working class that has no social consciousness). From the beginning, we [were] a more disciplined . . . force. They were very adventurous in their dealings with the police. We felt that they were shot through with [police] agents," Mike said. (According to the final Church Committee report, an "FBI extremist informant [was] involved in an intelligence investigation" of the Detroit BPP chapter in 1970, which led to the chapter's suspension by the BPP Central Committee. In 1972, when the chapter was reinstated, I joined it.)

The league also attempted an alliance with SNCC around

1969, when SNCC barely existed any more as a national organization. Mike became friends with James Forman, SNCC's longtime executive secretary. "SNCC was disintegrating, and Forman was looking for a place to go," Mike said. "[Forman] had some people, and we decided to merge. People in the league resented that. Forman had gotten a negative rap from some nationalists, and that followed him [to Detroit], and people were constantly undermining him. Of course, he was a very aggressive and assertive person, and he didn't help the situation."

As a Marxist-Leninist organization, the league was frequently at odds with Black Power era groups who opposed Marxism-Leninism. "It was important at that time that the idea of Marxism-Leninism be advanced," Mike said. "It was the liberating ideology for the Third World for a while. It was important that that be affirmed and reaffirmed here [in the United States]. It was also important for us to reaffirm the idea that the working class in this country had revolutionary potential. . . . The Panthers were saying the lumpen [had the potential]. The Students for a Democratic Society was saying students and elections. We said, no, that the working class was the revolutionary force in this country." According to Mike, the young people who were introduced to Marxism-Leninism were transformed: "They're some of the most accomplished people today that you can imagine."

The league's internal problems that Mike said he "could no longer abide" forced him to ultimately leave the organization. "I knew that the league was going to collapse because of the internal pressures as well as the external pressures from the police forces of the state. I felt that we had to expand in order to survive," Mike said. In addition, the Dodge Revolutionary Union Movement was harassed "on the street" by the FBI and had ideological and political differences with other Black Power organizations. "You have to remember that there were agents in all these organizations manipulating information back and forth. . . . You have a capitalist society with people filled with capitalist ideology. There were individual strivings and egos and ambitions and limited understanding and jealousies. Some people were rabid nationalists, and a lot of people who were not rabid nationalists were always vulnerable to manipulation by nationalists," Mike said.

He subsequently started the Black Workers Congress (BWC), of which he was the chairman and James Forman was the executive director. The group was composed of Black workers from around the country and disaffected SNCC members, Mike said. The BWC's headquarters was in Detroit, and there were chapters in fourteen cities. The group organized unions around the country, including in Atlanta, Birmingham, and Nashville. "We were very successful in places that had never been organized," Mike said. The BWC sponsored the National Black Economic Development Conference held in Detroit in April 1969. Ultimately, Mike said, internal and external pressures caused a split in the BWC, and it too collapsed.

Prior to and throughout the Black Power era, Black revolutionaries in several African countries waged armed liberation struggles to overthrow European colonial rule. These armed struggles were a source of great inspiration to many Black activists in the United States. Seeking to emulate Black freedom fighters in Africa, some Black activists in Los Angeles engaged in "weapon worship," said Joe Hicks. However, he added, some of these activists "didn't know which end [of a gun] the bullet came out of. I knew brothers who were just dangerous to be around because they had no training."

By 1968 Joe began to pull back from his work in the US organization. "I had begun to question what it was I thought I believed [and] some of the rigid black-and-white explanations of the world," he said. At the time, he explained, there was a sharp ideological debate going on in the Black Congress organization in LA among those members who believed in cultural nationalism and those who believed in revolutionary nationalism. The US organization was a leading proponent of cultural nationalism, which held that the reaffirmation of Black culture was central to Black Power. The BPP was a proponent of revolutionary nationalism, whose advocates believed that the best path for Black people to achieve their liberation was through a socialist revolution.

The FBI decided to exploit the ideological differences between the BPP and the US organization. According to the Church Committee report, in September 1968 FBI director J. Edgar Hoover ordered several Bureau field offices "to fully capitalize upon BPP and US differences . . . [by submitting] hard-hitting counterintelligence measures aimed at crippling the BPP." Those measures included sending fake anonymous letters in which Panthers and US members threatened violence against each other.

On January 17, 1969, Panthers and US members were among those who attended a meeting of Black students at the Los Angeles campus of the University of California. During the meeting, an altercation (whose origins remain in dispute to this day) occurred, and local Panther leaders Alprentice "Bunchy" Carter and John Huggins were shot to death. US members Larry Stiner, who was wounded during the incident, his brother George, and Donald

Hawkins were subsequently arrested and convicted of killing Bunchy and John.

Concerned about the ramifications of the "warfare" that had developed between the US organization and the Panthers, Joe said, "[I] broke [with US], just totally pulled out and said, 'I can't handle this.' The last year of my involvement with US was characterized by the struggle with the Panthers. [The struggle] was destructive to the [Black] movement. . . . I understand [the importance] of principled political disagreement, but when you start shooting folks down over these issues and [Blacks] have no power in the nation, there's something inherently perverted about that. . . . See, the struggle to me is something that [I] would be willing to lay my life down for, and I didn't see that at that point."

Advocates of Black Power had different views about white people, racism, and whether or not Blacks should work with their white "oppressors." These differing views caused a problem in Boston at the predominantly Black alternative New School for Children, where Joyce Grant was the principal in the late 1960s. The school had some white teachers and some white students. Joyce said that she encountered opposition from a Black couple who harassed the white teacher of one of their children. "[The Black parents] were very much into the Black Power movement," Joyce said. "This family felt because the school was a Black school in the Black community, there should [only] be Black teachers. I understood their perspective, but I couldn't accept it at the time because that was not the agreement [the school had made]." Due to the agreement, she supported the white teacher, and the Black parents tried to get her and the teacher fired. Joyce had the support of a majority of the teachers and parents, she said, but she subsequently resigned from the school.

In the San Francisco Bay Area, where Tanya Russell chaired an African Liberation Day (ALD) Committee in 1972 and 1973, she was criticized by some of the committee's Black members for her work in the Black Workers Congress, which advocated Marxism-Leninism. "There was clearly an anti–Marxist-Leninist line in the committee, and I was attacked for being in the BWC," Tanya said. "There was constant criticism of me from many in the group because I had a class [analysis] as well as a race analysis. We argued over terms. The Pan Africanists would say there was too much talk about imperialism. 'Let's just call it *white boys* and be done with it,' they would say. The ideological struggle ripped us apart."

Beginning in 1974 and continuing well into the 1980s, there were two Bay Area ALD celebrations annually—one organized by Black nationalists and the other by multiracial groups. According to Tanya, neither group was able to reach the numbers of Black people who had previously participated in ALD. Consequently, she did not participate in ALD after 1973. She said, "The conflict between extreme Black nationalism on the one hand and ultra-integration on the other was fatal to the movement."

For Tanya, the sexism she faced as the leader of the ALD committee was worse than the criticism she received for being a Marxist-Leninist. She recalled one committee meeting during which several Black men challenged her leadership so forcefully that she feared for her personal safety. Soon afterward, Tanya said, she put boards over the front door and windows of her house and started keeping guns in the house for protection. "That scared the heck out of my daughter. All we talked about was security, security, security."

Partly due to the resurgence of the feminist movement in the United States, a debate about the role of Black women in the Black liberation struggle erupted inside the Student Nonviolent Coordinating Committee in the late 1960s, a debate in which SNCC activist Frances Beal played a major role. By this time, her marriage had broken up, and she had moved with her two young daughters to New York City, where she worked in the SNCC campaign against the Vietnam War. The discussion that Frances and other SNCC women organized about the role of women concerned some very personal issues for her. She said, "In many ways, some of the oppression that I faced as a mother and in the home, the domestic side of it, was what drew me toward these big philosophical discussions." Recalling the opposition of some of the SNCC Black men to the discussion, Frances said, "The big criticism was, oh, this is just the white middle-class thing that has nothing to do with the liberty of Black women at all. . . . What we were grappling toward was that revolution wasn't just a male thing. . . . Our thing was really trying to win Black men to a revolutionary view on women."

Frances's paper "Slave of a Slave No More: Black Women in the Struggle" formed the basis of a proposal approved at a 1969 staff meeting to create a SNCC Black Women's Liberation Committee (BWLC), she said. By then, however, SNCC had virtually ceased to exist as a national organization, and "SNCC" was subsequently dropped from the BWLC's name. Many women who were not SNCC members joined the BWLC, which eventually became the Third World Women's Alliance, that Frances subsequently led.

In the late 1960s Lee Rose lived with her husband and three sons at the marine base at Camp Pendleton, California. "All the Black servicemen were giving the Black Power salute," she later recalled. "There were all these demonstrations in the streets against the Vietnam War. Something was happening every day. It was very exciting." For her, working with white people was a new experience. Born in the Jim Crow society of Texas and having grown up in Black neighborhoods in San Francisco, Lee had little preparation for working with young white students in the various multiracial coalitions in which she was active.

"Here I was in my early twenties, having had virtually no contact with whites. Then I was thrust into a situation where I had to cooperate with them," Lee said. Many of her Black activist friends would not cooperate with whites. "That was one of the things that caused friction between Blacks: whether or not you should be in a [multiracial] organization and accept assistance from whites, or whether you should you just go it alone. The Black movement was bombarded with [non-Black] people who wanted to help, to contribute. There were Black people who did not want this help. I saw that struggle destroy organizations," Lee said.

The National Welfare Rights Organization (NWRO), in which Jackie Pope was a leader, was founded in 1966 as a multiracial organization. However, the majority of the members, nationwide and in Brooklyn, where Jackie lived, were African American. "In its initial stages, the welfare rights movement was very conservative. We were totally separate from the Black Power movement," Jackie said. "Poor people are basically conservative folk. We still thought that the flag was wonderful, that this country could do no wrong, and that [welfare recipients] were poor because we were lazy and no good. It was a struggle [for the NWRO] to come out against the Vietnam War. The European American priests [who worked with us] were the ones who politicized us [about the welfare system]," Jackie said. The NWRO, most of whose members were women, did not escape the impact of the new Black consciousness in America. In the late 1960s, Jackie said, the white leaders of the group who had key positions were "purged" and replaced with people of color.

Elsewhere in Brooklyn, antisemitism became an issue for the Ocean Hill–Brownsville school board, which faced growing opposition from the largest teachers' union at the time in New York City, the United Federation of Teachers (UFT).

Many of the teachers in OHB schools were Jewish. In one instance, a pamphlet with antisemitic language that included the name of a Black Power activist who supported the OHB was distributed in the community, according to Rev. Oliver. He said that the activist knew nothing about the pamphlet and had not authorized the use of his name. Oliver blamed the incident on Albert Shanker, then the president of the UFT. "This is how they created the lie that the [OHB] board hated Jews," Oliver said.

Another problem for the movement for community-controlled schools in Brooklyn involved the employment of several parents in the schools. The administrator of the OHB school district hired several Black parents to work with the teachers, providing jobs for many low-income people. In return for higher pay, some of the Black parents agreed to support the UFT during the teachers' strike in the fall of 1968. "The majority of those Black parents joined with the union because they wanted more money," Oliver said. "It was divisive."

As a single working mother, Tanya Russell daily juggled the demands of being head of household and a political activist during the Black Power era. Often after leaving her job, she attended political meetings. Sometimes she had to take her daughter, who, according to Tanya, wished that her mother could be "a regular person." With her daughter in mind, Tanya eventually bought a house with a large dining room where meetings could be held. "We'd be arguing at my house at three or four o'clock in the morning about the revolution in the world. My child would be trying to sleep. . . . Looking back, I wouldn't do that again. I would have had a little more balance in my life," Tanya said.

Tanya was in her early thirties when she became a political activist. Many of her fellow activists were in their twenties, had never been married, and did not have children, she said. Consequently, Tanya said she "always felt sort of oppressed" as an activist. Nevertheless, she said she was determined that she was "*gonna* be in the movement or die trying." When she attended meetings of Black activists on the East Coast, Tanya said, many of the activists there were married men whose wives were not activists. "The wife would marry the guy thinking he was going to be a professional person and that was how their life was going to go. All of a sudden . . . he had his political awakening," Tanya said. "It probably led to a lot of divorces, I'm sure." According to Tanya, her activism caused friction with her family. "My family was pretty angry with the whole thing. To me, anybody who wasn't down with the movement was nothing. I was in my most idealistic moment. That was true for most [activists] I knew."

Like most of the women of color who were active in the National Welfare Rights Organization in Brooklyn,

Jackie Pope was a single mother. She recalled that a Catholic priest with whom the NWRO worked insisted that the group keep the office open on Thanksgiving to serve the community's poor. One Thanksgiving, the women rebelled and closed the office. "The theoreticians of the movement always wanted us to be out in the streets demonstrating," Jackie said. "I understood that . . . but we were parents. We had to [provide] a home for our kids. We were tired, and we couldn't always be out there. You just can't sustain that type of momentum." When she joined the NWRO's national staff in Washington, DC, in the late 1960s, Jackie frequently traveled in her work as editor of the NWRO newspaper and training coordinator for various programs, she said, leaving her four young daughters in the care of babysitters. So that her children could see where she was when she called home from the road, Jackie gave them a map.

Like Tanya's family, Jackie's family didn't understand her activism. "It was a long time before I could get my parents to see. They would talk about 'those welfare people' [and say] 'Why don't they . . . go get a job?' I said, 'You are talking about me.' They would say that I was different, but I would tell them, 'No, I'm not.' I saw this country for what it really is. I began to look at the issue of poverty and poor people in a whole different light. . . . I was no longer ashamed of getting public assistance."

During the Black Power era, Joyce Grant was single and had no children. "[The movement] totally consumed me. That's all I did," Joyce said. "It broke up my relationships with men who had other lives. They wanted my time, and I didn't want to give it to them. . . . You forget that there's another world, a world called 'work, pay the rent, have babies'. . . . [My experience] made me more sensitive and vulnerable as a woman. The relationships I had with men had to be of a particular nature. You want a mate that's going to share your energies and your interests."

At the height of the Black Power era, Lee Rose was a wife and the working mother of three young sons. At the time, she and her first husband, Earl Rose, who was also a political activist, took turns going to meetings and staying at home with their children, Lee said. "I dragged my children to a lot of rallies, and they were on picket lines with me. I am amazed that my kids came through that unscathed. They were never involved in gangs. They have respected young ladies all their lives, and they don't have any outside children." According to her, the movement didn't allow her and Earl to spend any private time together:

> There was always something to do. When you are involved in a movement, when you are driven by something and that something demands a lot of you, something is always sacrificed. When you are involved in a movement, that movement doesn't know a time schedule. It's like being a doctor when you have patients on call. You have people in your house all the time. . . . You have to learn about strategies and marches and building coalitions. Those things take time, especially when you are a novice, and your kids need to eat. Most people who considered themselves revolutionaries didn't take vacations.

After the Black Power era ended, Earl Rose lost his job at a Chicago-area General Motors plant where he had been a union activist. As a result, he and Lee lost their home. "[I lost] just about everything I had," Earl said. "It was very devastating. I was earning $10 to $12 an hour, a lot of money in those days. Lee was hardly making $6 to $7 an hour. I would sit there and say, 'My check is three times as big as yours.' I didn't say it with any malice, but now I understand the impact on her."

After over twenty years of marriage, the couple divorced. "We were struggling for something, but it was not congruently for each other," Earl said. "We didn't really have time to assess where we were at, keep in touch with each other. . . . [Lee] kinda felt that 'Earl's wife' thing, that she didn't have an identity. . . . I didn't understand where she was coming from. . . . I didn't understand how devastating that was for her. She was struggling within the women's movement and that kind of thing, and so we sort of went our separate ways. . . . So, when our kids graduated from high school and the movement was over, we looked at each other and said, 'What do we do now?'"

Rev. Oliver's leadership of the Ocean Hill–Brownsville movement for community control of schools kept him away from home nearly all of the time "for months and months," he said. "[The OHB board] affected my family life. There were times when my former wife felt that I was not giving enough time to her and the children, giving too much time to other things. That may have contributed to our eventual divorce. It was a busy time for me for a good four years, just constant going day and night. . . . I ran myself down in 1968 during the [teachers'] strike. . . . There are some people who if they hear the name 'Rev. C. Herbert Oliver' close the door."

His political activism also caused members of his family to lose their jobs, Oliver said. According to him, his first wife worked for a Jewish attorney who fired her after Rev.

Oliver testified on behalf of a Puerto Rican principal whom a Jewish group accused of antisemitism. "[My wife] was doing well [working for the attorney]. He had no complaint with her. She just got fired without cause." After he and his first wife were divorced, he remarried. He said that his second wife was "fired or blocked from at least a dozen positions" because of his role in the OHB movement. In addition, his brother and sister were fired from their jobs when their employers discovered that they were related to him, Oliver said.

Likewise, Republic of New Africa activist Che Parker often spent more time "with the movement" than with his family, Che said. "I had a couple of kids outside of marriage, and that may have been one reason why my family situation kind of failed. It wasn't my intent to impregnate the sisters, but it was just part of the thing at the time, you know, building the tribes." Che said, "I didn't have much social life. I look back on it now and think about all the music and the dancing and the fashions and the travel that I could have been doing, and those days just passed me by. I really didn't expect to live to be thirty years old. . . . You can just about forget having a personal life when you're in the struggle. . . . It's just that when you're that focused, everything else just kind of seems irrelevant." Furthermore, Che said, "We were under pressure from the power structure. . . . Not only were we dodging from white folks, but there were some elderly people in our own neighborhoods who were turning us in and calling the police on us, figuring that they were doing what was right and what we were doing was wrong." One exception to this was Che's mother, whom he said was always proud of him and very supportive of his activism.

After Father Neil allowed the Black Panther Party to meet in his Episcopal church in Oakland, "there were many lonely times," he said.

> Even some of the progressive Black clergy questioned what some said was a foolish thing to do. . . . Living through the Black Power period helped me to deal with being lonely. . . . The movement fostered and nurtured my commitment against injustice. . . . It was a continuing growing thing for me. My commitment was heightened when I was dealing with racism in the structure of the [Episcopal] Church. I saw the whole thing from a theological basis . . . [it] was the call of the Gospel. I feel just like that song, "I can see clearly now". . . . My involvement in the Black Power movement helped me foster a view of life that you only come this way once, and you have to set priorities for yourself, what's important, and not be afraid to take risks and not be afraid to be misunderstood.

CHAPTER 6

Serving the People

The Survival Programs of the Black Panther Party

While speaking about the Black Panther Party to college students in a Black American literature class, I was reminded once again that the establishment news media, historians, and political scientists have not provided a full treatment of the BPP. The students (of various ethnic backgrounds) with whom I spoke were surprised yet pleased to learn that the Black Panthers fed hungry children, escorted senior citizens to banks to cash their checks, administered a model elementary school, and tested people for sickle cell anemia, the rare blood disease. Unfortunately, these community service activities lacked the sensationalism of the gun battles between police and BPP members. Not surprisingly, the only recollection of the BPP for many of the students was the party's confrontations with law enforcement officials. Heretofore, the Panther survival programs have received minimal popular and scholarly attention.

First, this chapter addresses the theoretical underpinnings of the survival programs. Second, the specific projects constituting the survival programs are described, and finally the impact of the survival programs is assessed. From 1972 to 1981, as a member of the Black Panther Party and the last editor of the *Black Panther Intercommunal News Service,* I participated in many of the various survival programs and knew the importance of these service projects to their recipients. I hope that this essay proves useful to contemporary young African American activists.

Theoretical Underpinnings

A key philosophical pillar of the Black Power era of 1965–1975 was the concept of Black self-determination. In the classic treatise *Black Power: The Politics of Liberation in America,* Black Power theorists Kwame Ture (formerly Stokely Carmichael) and Charles V. Hamilton wrote, “Black people in America must get themselves together. [Black Power] is about black people taking care of business—the business of and for black people. . . . If we succeed, we will exercise control over our lives, politically, economically and psychically.” To gain such control, Ture and Hamilton urged Black communities to develop experimental programs “out of day-to-day work, out of interaction between organizers and the communities in which they work.” The Black Panther Party’s survival programs rested on this idea of self-determination. Panthers established a network of community service projects designed to improve the life chances of African American people. Institutional racism relegated a disproportionate number of African Americans to deplorable housing, poor health care services, an unresponsive criminal justice system, inadequate diets, and substandard education. The party’s survival programs aimed to help Black people overcome the devastating effects of racism and capitalism. Panther officials explained, “The programs, which cover such diverse areas as health care and food services as well as a model school, the Intercommunal Youth Institute, are meant to meet the needs of the community until we all can move to change social conditions that make it impossible for the people to afford the things they need and desire."

In 1971 these community service projects were formally defined as survival programs by Huey P. Newton. However, long before this official pronouncement, many of the specific projects of the survival programs were originally developed by various Panther affiliates to meet the immediate needs of their respective communities. For example, the party's armed police patrols in Oakland dated back to October 1966, while the Seattle branch initiated one of the early free breakfast programs in 1968.

Political activism constitutes the second pillar undergirding the party's survival programs. Newton placed a premium on political action to organize the community. He recalled, "When we formed the Party, we did so because we wanted to put theory and practice together in a systematic manner." The desire to serve and empower African American people guided the operations of the survival programs. Dr. Kim Kit Holder, former New York Panther, writes in his dissertation, "The BPP believed that by setting an example with their survival programs they could serve the people as well as demonstrate to them the method of developing people's (community-controlled) institutions." Critics, however, contend that the party abandoned its original revolutionary objective with the adoption of the survival programs. Bobby Seale countered this misperception: "A lot of people misunderstand the politics of these programs; some people have a tendency to call them reform programs. They're not reform programs; they're actually revolutionary community programs. A revolutionary program is one set forth by revolutionaries, by those who want to change the existing system to a better system. A reform program is set up by the existing exploitative system as an appeasing handout to fool the people and keep them quiet."

Huey Newton explained further, "We called them survival programs pending revolution. . . . They were designed to help the people survive until their consciousness is raised, which is only the first step in the revolution to produce a new America. . . . During a flood the raft is a life-saving device, but it is only a means of getting to higher ground. So, too, with survival programs, which are emergency services. In themselves they do not change social conditions, but they are life-saving vehicles until conditions change."

Nevertheless, Newton's decision to emphasize community service projects did create intra-organizational strife in 1971. Some members, including Eldridge Cleaver, favored an offensive military policy over the self-help activities of the survival programs. This tactical disagreement, which was exacerbated by the FBI's counterintelligence program, ultimately led to the death of several party members. From 1966 to 1982, the BPP instituted a host of specific community service projects. The survival projects included police-alert patrols, the *Black Panther Intercommunal News Service*, the free breakfast for children program, free medical clinics, the Oakland Community School, free busing to prisons, the free food program, the free clothing and shoes programs, the free ambulance program, sickle cell anemia testing, Seniors Against a Fearful Environment (SAFE), and the free pest-control program. These various community activities are easily categorized into four social policy areas: human sustenance, health, education, and criminal justice.

Human Sustenance

In order to fully develop the human capital of a community, the day-to-day needs of the people must be addressed. Party members understood that in order to maximize one's potential, personal safety, nourishment, and adequate health care were paramount. Unfortunately, for many African Americans, this was not the case. Consequently, the BPP implemented programs to enhance the life chances of the impoverished sector of the African American community. In one of his early political statements, "In Defense of Self-Defense," Newton described the relationship between politics and the material needs of the Black community: "The masses of Black people have always been deeply entrenched and involved in the basic necessities of life. They have not had time to abstract their situation. Abstractions come only with leisure. The people have not had the luxury of leisure. Therefore, the people have been very aware of the true definition of politics: politics are merely the desire of individuals and groups to satisfy first, their basic needs—food, shelter and clothing, and security for themselves and their loved ones."

Classical philosophers such as Thomas Hobbes note the importance of personal and group security in the formation of the polity. The party underscored this critical need when it formed the police-alert patrols in 1966. The first and perhaps the most controversial survival program, the police-alert patrol, aimed to counter the pervasive police brutality in the Black community of Oakland. Indeed, the eradication of police brutality was the catalyst that led to the formation of the Black Panther Party for Self-Defense in 1966. As noted in chapter 3, point seven of the BPP platform demanded "an immediate end to POLICE BRUTALITY and MURDER of Black people" and urged African Americans to form armed self-defense groups to fight "racist police oppression and brutality."

In 1966 California statute permitted an individual to carry a loaded gun in public as long as it was not concealed and did not have a bullet in the chamber. Huey, Bobby, and other Panthers—armed with loaded weapons, cameras, law books, and tape recorders—monitored the police in the Black community of Oakland. These Panther community patrols prevented incidents of police harassment and advised detained suspects of their legal rights. An avid student of the law, Huey gained a reputation for facing down police officers with a loaded shotgun and for his mastery of the law. The police patrols gained the party notoriety and respect in the Black community. Of course, this activity also earned the enmity of the police. Furthermore, the police-alert patrols served as a recruiting mechanism during the BPP's formative years. The party's success in Richmond, California, is a case in point. In April 1967 twenty-two-year-old Denzil Dowell was shot to death by a deputy sheriff in Richmond. The Dowell family asked the Panthers to investigate the death, which was officially ruled a justifiable homicide. The party organized a series of rallies in which a delegation of "twenty Panthers out there armed with guns, disciplined, standing thirty or forty feet apart on every corner of the intersection were in full view of the local police." Seale recalled, "We were educating the people that we would die for them. This was the position we always took with brother Huey P. Newton." He further reported, "Just about everybody out there joined the Party that day."

An extension of the party's original vision to defend the Black community was the creation of the Seniors Against a Fearful Environment (SAFE) program. The safety of senior citizens was at great peril. One study reported that over a six-week period "of the combined total of 249 victims of strongarm robbery and purse snatching, 48 percent of the victims (118) were over the age of fifty." During Bobby Seale's 1972–1973 mayoral campaign and Elaine Brown's city council bid, the BPP initiated the SAFE program. In response to a request from a group of senior citizens, the BPP provided free transportation and an escort service. These services permitted the elderly to cash their Social Security and pension checks as well as take care of other monthly errands. When the program started, Seale announced, "The Black Panther Party is demanding that muggers and would-be muggers stop these acts. We're calling upon the community to support the program and look out for the welfare of our elderly citizens; if it had not been for senior citizens, we would not be here." SAFE successfully lobbied the Oakland City Housing Authority to make major repairs and clean up a low-income residence for senior citizens in downtown Oakland.

Party members mobilized and empowered people by ensuring that the community was informed. Emory Douglas, former BPP minister of culture, recounted, "Huey compared the party's need for a publication with the armed struggle of the Vietnamese. He said that the Vietnamese carried mimeograph machines wherever they went to produce flyers and other literature to spread the word about their fight to free their country. The party needed to have a newspaper so we could tell our own story." Published April 25, 1967, the inaugural issue of the party's newspaper, the *Black Panther Community News Service*, was a four-page mimeographed sheet devoted to the death of Denzil Dowell and police brutality in Black America. First published monthly, the *Black Panther* became a weekly publication in January 1968. The combative editorial of the first issue of the *Black Panther* set the tone of the newspaper for the next four years. After listing the "questionable facts" concerning the police shooting of Denzil Dowell, the editorial stated: "The white cop is the instrument sent into our community by the Power structure to keep Black people quiet and under control . . . it is time that Black People start moving in a direction that will free our communities from this form of outright brutal oppression. The BLACK PANTHER PARTY FOR SELF-DEFENSE has worked out a program that is carefully designed to cope with this situation."

Eldridge Cleaver, one of the BPP's most controversial leaders, was the first editor of the *Black Panther*. In December 1966, two months after the founding of the party, he was paroled from prison as the author of the critically acclaimed, national bestseller, *Soul on Ice*. Several months later, Huey invited Eldridge to join the BPP, and Cleaver subsequently became the party's minister of information. During Cleaver's editorship, the *Black Panther* reflected his provocative manner. In one article in which Eldridge criticized the police, whom the Panthers called "pigs," Eldridge wrote: "A dead pig is desirable, but a paralyzed pig is preferable to a mobile pig. . . . In order to stop the slaughter of the people we must accelerate the slaughter of the pigs." The depiction of the police as pigs, generally regarded as dirty, odious animals, was a calculated attempt by the BPP to use words to politicize the Black community and sympathetic whites. Influenced by the German philosopher Friedrich Nietzsche, who believed that concepts of good and evil are used by those in power to maintain control over the powerless, Huey Newton and the BPP employed "a form of psychological warfare [that] raised the consciousness of the people and also inflicted a new consciousness of the ruling circle."

As described in chapter 3, provocative articles and cartoons drawn by Emory Douglas and other party artists, which illustrated the police as pigs, brought the *Black Panther* under close government scrutiny. In a May 15, 1970, memorandum, FBI Director J. Edgar Hoover declared that the BPP's newspaper was "one of the most effective propaganda operations of the BPP. . . . It is the voice of the BPP and if it could be effectively hindered, it would result in helping to cripple the BPP." Hoover had cause for concern. By 1970, the weekly circulation of the *Black Panther* surpassed 100,000 copies. It sold for twenty-five cents per copy and was a major revenue resource for the organization. Less than a week after Hoover's memo, the San Diego FBI office proposed to spray a foul-smelling chemical on copies of the *Black Panther*. In September 1970 the US House of Representatives Committee on Internal Security investigated the newspaper.

By March 1978 when I became the editor of the *Black Panther*, the membership of the BPP had declined significantly from a high of five thousand members to less than a couple dozen Panthers. Similarly, the newspaper experienced a significant reduction in personnel from thirteen members in 1974, when I first joined the newspaper staff, to six members in 1978. The reduction in the size of the staff and dwindling finances eventually reduced the frequency of the production of the newspaper. It was a weekly publication until 1978. After this the paper experienced sporadic production and ceased publication in 1980. Nevertheless, the *Black Panther* consistently maintained a militant stance on issues affecting Black and poor people. It offered readers an alternative to the mainstream media. One such example was the *Black Panther*'s coverage of the Jonestown tragedy. In November 1978 more than nine hundred Americans, most of whom were Black and members of the People's Temple, a San Francisco church led by Rev. Jim Jones, allegedly committed suicide in Guyana. The staff of the *Black Panther* spent six exhaustive weeks investigating the incident and dedicated an entire issue of the paper to what we described as the Jonestown massacre.

Perhaps the most respected and popular of the survival programs was the free breakfast for schoolchildren. Several Bay Area branches, as well as the Seattle branch of the BPP, established free breakfast programs in 1968. The following year this survival project was nearly uniformly adopted by other party affiliates in compliance with a 1969 organizational directive issued by Chairman Seale. In addition to selling the party's newspaper, the breakfast for children program was a mainstay of party affiliates. Party chapters in Oakland and New York offered breakfast at multiple sites. Teams of Panthers served a no-frills breakfast of eggs, grits, toast, and bacon to children before the school day started. Churches nationwide hosted the party's breakfast programs. Father Neil in Oakland maintained, "Black preachers have got to stop preaching about a kingdom in the hereafter which is a 'land flowing with milk and honey'. . . . We must deal with concrete conditions and survival in this life! The Black Panther Party . . . has merely put into operation the survival program that the Church should have been doing anyway. The efforts of the Black Panther Party are consistent with what God wants."

BPP members solicited financial contributions from community residents and food donations from local businesses to sponsor its breakfast program. Many parents and other community residents volunteered to help implement the project.

In addition to ensuring that young children received a meal before attending school, the BPP sought to raise public consciousness about hunger and poverty in America. Seale told his audiences, "[There are] millions of people . . . who are living below subsistence; welfare mothers, poor white people, . . . Latinos, and black people. This type of program, if spread out, should readily relate to the needs of the people." Moreover, the party linked the importance of adequate nourishment and educational performance when it asked, "How can our children learn anything when most of their stomachs are empty?" Party members fed thousands of hungry children each school day throughout the nation. This community service program no doubt enhanced the stature of the party. A *Wall Street Journal* story reported, "A sizable number of Blacks support the Panthers because they admire . . . less-publicized activities of the party such as its free breakfast programs for ghetto youngsters, its free medical care program and its war on narcotics use among black youth." Success of the breakfast program attracted the attention of the FBI and became a primary target of the FBI counterintelligence program. The FBI sent letters to church members discouraging the use of their church for the breakfast programs. Store merchants were dissuaded from donating to the breakfast program, while FBI media leaks accused the party of extortion to finance the free breakfast project and brainwashing school-age children with antiwhite propaganda.

An outgrowth of feeding hungry children was the party's exposure to other pressing needs of community residents. For example, former BPP member Assata Shakur (formerly Joanne Chesimard) recalled working in the breakfast program in New York City's East Harlem: "In the middle of winter some of the kids were without hats, gloves, scarves, and boots and wore just some skimpy coats or jackets. When it was possible, we tried to hook them up with something free from the clothing drive." Impoverished adults in the community also lacked basic necessities. Consequently, the party instituted a number of free programs that involved the distribution of food, shoes, and clothing. During a 1972 community survival conference, the Panthers distributed more than ten thousand free bags of groceries during the three-day affair. Party members eventually established a food bank to store food needed for periodic mass distributions. In addition, members of the BPP launched massive free shoe and free clothing giveaways. Following his release from prison in May 1971, Bobby Seale returned to Oakland and took charge of the survival programs. Elaine Brown would remember, "He [Seale] created the most magnificent food giveaways. The big ones became major community events, even reported in the media. . . . Bobby organized a campaign to give away bags of groceries to whole families, with a stalking panther printed on each bag. The community and the press went wild. Bobby's giant food giveaways begat tremendous support for all our other Survival Programs. Even middle-class Blacks, heretofore, reluctant to support or be identified with the party, began endorsing it and making contributions."

Health Programs

Panther activism extended to health concerns as well. Members of the BPP sponsored three major programs to address the lack of adequate health services in the Black community. Health-related survival projects included free health clinics, sickle cell anemia testing, and a free ambulance service. Since the party's health programs required medical workers and equipment, the health projects were not as plentiful as some of the other survival programs. One of the first efforts to implement Chairman Seale's 1969 directive to institute free health clinics was undertaken by the Kansas City, Missouri, branch of the Black Panther Party, which opened the Bobby Hutton Community Clinic on August 20, 1969. Soon afterward party branches in Brooklyn, Boston, Cleveland, Philadelphia, Seattle, Chicago, and Rockford, Illinois, created free health clinics. Although medical cadres in the party received first aid training, the survival of the clinics depended on health professional s, such as Dr. Tolbert Small of Oakland, to donate their time. The health clinics offered a variety of services, including first aid, physical examinations, prenatal care, and testing for lead poisoning, high blood pressure, and sickle cell anemia. An exemplary party health clinic operated by the Panthers was the Spurgeon "Jake" Winters People's Free Medical Care Center established in Chicago in January 1970 by the Illinois chapter of the BPP. Dr. Holder writes, "The clinic served over 2,000 people within the first two months of its existence." Medical teams from the Winters clinic went door-to-door assisting people with their health problems; the clinic's staff included obstetricians, gynecologists, pediatricians, and general practitioners.

Sickle cell anemia testing was another major health community service program offered by the Black Panther Party. Panthers were at the forefront of an educational and medical campaign to eradicate sickle cell anemia, a rare blood disease that primarily affects people of African descent. In a front-page article in the *Black Panther*, "Black Genocide, Sickle Cell Anemia," the party accused the US government of refusing to conduct research to find a cure for the disease. Five weeks after the publication of this article, the BPP announced that its medical clinics would begin free testing for sickle cell anemia and the sickle cell trait. The Jake Winters Medical Center conducted the party's first sickle cell testing in May 1971, testing about six hundred children in a three-day period. In Houston, the BPP trained Texas Southern University students and community residents to perform testing for sickle cell anemia, hypertension, and diabetes. According to David Hilliard, BPP chief of staff, the party "established nine free testing clinics, publicizing the problem so successfully that [President] Nixon mention[ed] sickle cell in that year's health message to Congress."

The Joseph Waddell People's Free Ambulance Service, established in early 1974 by the Winston-Salem, North Carolina, branch of the BPP, was another health venture of the party. Panthers in Winston-Salem were granted a franchise by the Forsyth County commissioners and financed their ambulance service with a grant awarded by the national office of the Episcopal Church. It included twenty-four-hour service, with a voluntary staff of twenty certified members who received extensive emergency medical technician training. The ambulance service operated for two years.

Educational Programs

From the party's inception, its leaders attacked what they considered to be a biased and distorted educational process. Hence, the demand for a relevant education was explicitly stated in the organization's Ten-Point Platform and Program. Point five stated: "We want education for our people that exposes the true nature of this decadent American society. We want education that teaches us our true history and our role in the present-day society." The BPP sought to overcome the problem of substandard education with the creation of liberation schools, community political education classes, and the Intercommunal Youth Institute. As early as 1969, the various affiliates of the Black Panther Party instituted liberation schools. Members of the Berkeley branch instituted one of the first liberation schools on June 25, 1969.

According to chairman Bobby Seale, liberation schools taught children "about the class struggle in terms of black history." The lesson plans of these schools included presentations on party activities, Black history, and current events. Students usually received breakfast and lunch during their attendance of the liberation schools, which "were an outgrowth of the interaction with children of the FBP [Free Breakfast Program]. Frustrated with the lack of time to talk with children, many Panthers were eager to establish liberation schools." Unfortunately, government officials were sometimes successful in convincing community leaders and parents not to cooperate with the party. Consequently, in some cities, including Omaha and Des Moines, the school program was discontinued. The party's community political education classes were the educational counterpart for adults. In addition to listening to lectures about the party's ideology, goals, and activities, community adults were taught basic reading and writing skills.

The key educational component of the party's survival programs was the Intercommunal Youth Institute. In January 1971, the Oakland chapter established the Intercommunal Youth Institute (later renamed the Oakland Community School, in 1974). According to the party, giving rationale for the school's establishment, "We understand clearly that those who can control the mind can control the body. What we have is an educational system which is completely controlled by the power structure." At the beginning, there were twenty-eight students in the school, many of whom were the children of BPP members. Students ages two-and-a-half to eleven attended the institute. They were placed in levels instead of grades, and their placement was made according to their abilities rather than age. Therefore, a student might be in a fourth-level math class but in a first-level English or reading class. Meals were provided, and buses transported the pupils to and from school as well as to medical and dental appointments. During the fall of 1973, the Youth Institute was housed in a former church in East Oakland's predominantly Black community. The school graduated its first class in June 1974. At one point, there were four hundred children on its waiting list. Ericka

Huggins served as the director of the school from 1973 to 1981. In September 1977, California governor Edmund "Jerry" Brown Jr. and the California legislature gave the Oakland Community School a special award for "having set the standard for the highest level of elementary education in the state." The last class graduated from the school in 1982. (Former party member Carol Granison and I wrote the school's curriculum for language arts, which I taught.)

Criminal Justice Programs

The 1966 version of the BPP Ten-Point Platform and Program included two demands concerning the US criminal justice system. Point eight demanded, "We want freedom for all Black men held in federal, state, county, and city prisons and jails." In a similar vein, point nine demanded, "We want all black people when brought to trial to be tried in court by a jury of their peer group or people from their black communities, as defined by the Constitution of the United States." In the early days of the organization, the party informed community residents of their constitutional rights. Early issues of the *Black Panther* included a column by Huey P. Newton, "Pocket Lawyer of Legal First Aid," which noted, "[Black people] are always the first to be arrested and the racist police forces are constantly trying to pretend that rights are extended equally to all people. Cut [the "Pocket Lawyer"] out, brothers and sisters, and carry it with you . . . at all time[s] remember the fifth amendment. . . . Do not resist arrest under any circumstances. . . . Do not engage in 'friendly' conversation with officers." For a time, the BPP newspaper also included a section that explained state and federal gun laws.

Established in Seattle in July 1970, the party's free busing-to-prisons program provided transportation for families and friends to visit their relatives who were incarcerated. Seattle BPP members recalled, "We found out that many families and friends cannot afford transportation to these prisons to visit their loved ones. The result is that the prisoners feel that no one even cares about them. . . . [The busing program provided] a chance to establish some type of communication between the community and the prisoners." This program was one of the first survival projects in which I personally participated after joining the Detroit branch of the BPP in 1972. I drove one of the vans that transported families to visit their incarcerated relatives at Michigan's Jackson State Prison. Having grown up as the sheltered daughter of a minister and a music teacher, I was overwhelmed by my experience at Jackson State Prison, which was my first visit to a penitentiary. Another service that the BPP provided for prison inmates was the free commissary program. BPP members secured donations of personal hygiene items and nonperishable foods and sent care packages to prisoners. The party also offered attorney referral services for inmates.

Legacy of the Survival Programs

Sociologist Herbert H. Haines has suggested that the activities and rhetoric of Black Power groups like the Black Panther Party provided a "positive radical flank" for Black progress. According to Haines, Black radicals of the 1960s improved the bargaining position of mainstream civil rights groups, which hastened the accomplishment of many of their goals. There is evidence that the BPP's survival programs contributed not only to the improved bargaining position of civil rights groups but also for all poor people in America. First, in the area of police-community relations, the party's police-alert patrols educated the public about police brutality. In Oakland, the Panthers increased public awareness about the role and actions of the police. A Citizens' Complaint Board to hear allegations of police abuse was established by the Oakland City Council in 1981—fourteen years after the BPP launched its community patrols of the police.

Contemporary incidents of police brutality (such as the Rodney King case, among others) demonstrate that police abuse of African Americans continues. Nonetheless, today, unlike the 1960s, "three strikes and you're out" is the prevailing public attitude toward criminals. This attitude is perhaps understandable, given the rapid growth during the 1980s and 1990s in the sale and use of crack cocaine and its attendant violent crime. Given the contemporary situation, the BPP's call in 1966 for the "immediate" release of all Blacks in prisons and jails would understandably draw little support. Nevertheless, the party's observations that Black and poor people are not tried by a jury of their peers and that crime and poverty are inextricably linked remain correct.

The BPP's breakfast program and food giveaways also raised public consciousness about hunger and poverty in the United States. The precursor to the present national free school lunch program, the party's free breakfast for children survival program was a popular community service activity. Indeed, Panther activism provides a model of community self-help. Finally, in the area of education, the Black Panther Party established the Oakland Community School in 1971 as an alternative to the substandard education foisted on the city's low-income and working-class children. However, Oakland must not be singled out. Then, as now, public education is in crisis throughout the United States, particularly in large, urban school districts. Notwithstanding the sincere efforts of parents and teachers to improve education, urban schools are often abandoned. Is it not possible to create Oakland Community Schools throughout America?

Nearly sixty years have elapsed since Huey P. Newton and Bobby Seale founded the Black Panther Party. Despite the passage of time, however, the party's quest for "land, bread, housing, education, clothing, justice and peace" remains elusive for far too many Black and poor people in America. Consequently, in recent years there has been a renewed interest in the BPP, particularly by African American youth. Several former Panthers have written books about their experiences, young artists have rapped about the party, and a major motion picture on the BPP has been produced. What are our young people, who are searching for role models, to make of the sometimes-contradictory accounts of the Black Panther Party?

Above all, it must be remembered that the BPP was an organization composed of young African Americans from diverse social and economic backgrounds. Moreover, party affiliates throughout the country possessed distinct organizing styles and programs based on the qualities of the local membership and the particular needs of their respective communities. What happened in one chapter of the party did not necessarily occur in the same manner in another chapter. Furthermore, members of the BPP were young men and women, many in our teens and twenties. There were undoubtedly times when members of the BPP romanticized the Black liberation struggle. As a result, we seriously underestimated the apparatus of the state in the most powerful country in the world. Moreover, we did not always operate democratically and sometimes failed to fully grasp the imperatives of leadership. Last, but certainly not least, the BPP was the main target of the FBI's counterintelligence program to destroy the entire Black Power movement. The pervasive government repression directed against the party affected all aspects of organizational life. It developed an atmosphere of mistrust and personal danger among the members. In the end, the Panthers sought to transform powerless Black and poor people into powerful political individuals in their attempt to actualize the motto of the Black Panther Party, "All Power to the People." As Huey P. Newton recalled, "We knew that this strategy would raise the consciousness of the people and also give us their support . . . revolution is a process . . . we offered [the programs] as a vehicle to move [the people] to a higher level. . . . In their quest for freedom . . . they have to see first some basic accomplishments, in order to realize that major successes are possible."

CHAPTER 7

"The Party Was Irresistible"

Brutality by white police officers against poor Black people in America's inner cities was a key factor in many of the Black rebellions of the 1960s, including those in Detroit, Newark, and Los Angeles. In Oakland, the local police department recruited several white, southern-born officers—many of whom brought their racist attitudes toward Blacks to their new jobs. On October 15, 1966, two college students in Oakland, Huey P. Newton and Bobby Seale, decided that it was time for Blacks to organize against police brutality and founded the Black Panther Party for Self-Defense.

Like many young Blacks at the time, Huey, twenty-four, and Bobby, twenty-nine, who had been friends since 1962, were influenced by the sentiments of Black Power then sweeping across America. The two men, born in the South, came from working-class Black families who moved to Oakland during World War II. Huey's family came from Louisiana and Bobby's from Texas. The youngest of seven children, Huey was sometimes in trouble with the law during his adolescence. Frequently expelled from school, he was unable to read when he graduated from high school—a problem he overcame with the help of an older brother.

Bobby, the oldest of three children, was a high school dropout who served in the air force for three years before being dishonorably discharged. He later worked as a sheet metal mechanic in the aerospace industry. In the fall of 1966, Huey and Bobby were students at Oakland City College (now Merritt College), where they were members of such groups as the Afro-American Association and the Soul Students Advisory Council. They also belonged to an off-campus Black Power group, the Northern California branch of the Revolutionary Action Movement. (As noted in chapter 1, RAM was one of the groups targeted in 1967 for disruption by the FBI's COINTELPRO.)

When the BPP started, it was legal for people to carry unconcealed guns in California. Huey, Bobby, and their recruits, typically with shotguns strapped to their shoulders, attracted attention throughout the San Francisco Bay Area during their "community patrols" of the police. Black Panthers monitored police conduct and advised people who were arrested or harassed of their legal rights. White officials of the power structure of California, no doubt terrified at the sight of armed Black men challenging the authority of the police, struck back against the BPP. A bill, designed to disarm the fledgling Black Panthers, was proposed in the California legislature to make it illegal for an unlicensed person to carry a concealed or an unconcealed gun in a public place. Some thirty armed Black Panthers, including Bobby Seale, marched into the state capitol in Sacramento on May 2, 1967, to protest the bill, which was later passed. Until then, the BPP was largely unknown outside of the San Francisco Bay Area. That changed after the protest in Sacramento, which made national news.

In October 1967, a year after the BPP was founded, Huey

was arrested for killing a white police officer and seriously wounding another one after the two Oakland cops stopped a car in which Huey was a passenger. The BPP cofounder was also seriously injured during the incident, and a picture of him handcuffed to a hospital gurney made national news. Claiming that the two Oakland cops had tried to murder Huey, the BPP began a campaign to get him out of jail. Thousands of young Blacks across America subsequently joined the party. Overseas, Black, white, and Third World progressive and radical groups took up the demand: "Free Huey." Originally charged with murder, Huey was convicted in September 1968 of voluntary manslaughter in the death of police officer John Frey. Just days before Huey's conviction, FBI Director J. Edgar Hoover declared war on the BPP, calling it "the greatest threat to the internal security of the country." Subsequently, the party and Huey were added to the FBI's list of "black-nationalist hate groups and their leaders," and the BPP became the main target of the FBI's counterintelligence program against the Black liberation movement. According to the 1976 report by the US Senate's Church Committee that investigated intelligence abuses, 233 of the 295 documented FBI COINTELPRO actions against the Black liberation movement between 1967 and 1969 were undertaken against the BPP. "Although the claimed purpose of the Bureau's COINTELPRO tactics was to prevent violence, some of the FBI's tactics against the BPP were clearly intended to foster violence," the report determined.

Huey was released from prison in August 1970 after his conviction was overturned. In 1969, Bobby was arrested after he and seven white political activists (originally known as the Chicago Eight) were indicted for conspiracy to incite a riot and other charges related to protests at the Democratic National Convention in Chicago in August 1968. Eventually tried separately from the white activists, Bobby was convicted, but his conviction was later overturned. Meanwhile, he and thirteen other Panthers were charged with the May 1969 murder of Panther Alex Rackley in New Haven, Connecticut. In 1971 Bobby was acquitted.

Much of the early attention on the BPP focused on its belief that Black people had a right to arm themselves against police brutality and government repression. However, the party's Ten-Point Platform and Program also demanded decent education, housing, and health care for Black people; fair treatment in the criminal justice system; and full employment. Beginning in 1968, BPP chapters around the country provided several free community services, called survival programs, as described in chapter 6.

Melvin Dickson, like Huey and Bobby, was a student at Oakland City College in the fall of 1966. Born in 1940 in West Memphis, Arkansas, Melvin joined the US Navy in 1959 shortly after graduating from high school. During the four years he was a sailor, he was based a few miles from Oakland at the naval air station in Alameda, California, where he spent most of his time when he was on leave. "I was like most people who joined the service, looking for opportunities and some excitement. You join the navy and see the world," Melvin said. Discharged from the navy in June 1963, he settled in Oakland, planning to work while using the GI Bill to go back to school to improve his skills.

After President John F. Kennedy was assassinated in November 1963, Melvin said, "I started to pay attention to what was going on and read the paper more. That had some impact on me because Kennedy was a supporter of civil rights. Even before the Black Panther Party, the organization I began to notice was the Nation of Islam. I used to read their papers. Of course, I had problems with their religious thing, but they pointed to something that at that time made a lot of sense, in terms of how [Black people] began to look at themselves. Malcolm X [the national spokesman for the Nation of Islam until December 1963] was pretty vocal at the time. I was hanging out in the streets, in the fast life. I was living on the streets and trying to go to school, and I was kind of split. I was identifying with Malcolm. I was following his lifestyle. I thought I was gonna become another Malcolm X. That hustler life had appeal to it. When Malcolm was assassinated, it really changed how I looked at the Black Power movement. I was affected just like all the other folks around here."

From 1964 to 1967, Melvin worked as a driver for a retail outlet and delivered milk "all over . . . the whole black community" in the East Bay area. His roommate had gone to public school with Huey, and Melvin saw the BPP cofounder around the Bay Area several times before the two men were formally introduced on October 27, 1967. The next day, Huey was arrested for killing police officer John Frey and shooting officer Herbert Heanes. "When I heard about [it], it blew my mind," Melvin said. "Before that, I didn't take serious note of [the BPP]. Huey had an advanced understanding of politics, you know, unlike many other folks. He could articulate the things that you thought you identified with. And that's what impressed me." Melvin was friends with some people who were close to the party, and he started attending the BPP's Free Huey rallies. "The party was irresistible. I was identifying with Huey because I felt pretty much like he did. When I graduated from high school, I was semi-illiterate. I had basic reading and math skills, but I wanted to improve myself." After Huey's arrest, Melvin said, "I totally gave up running the streets. I got married, got more serious about politics, and [tried] to sharpen myself up a little."

When he went to the BPP office to join the group, Melvin was told the party wasn't accepting new members. So, sometime in 1969, he and his wife moved to Seattle where there was a Panther chapter. "The same day we got there, we went straight to the Black Panther Party," Melvin said. They initially did volunteer work, including selling the party's newspaper. Seattle Panthers also ran free community services, including a breakfast program for children, a busing-to-prisons program, and a health clinic. At the clinic, people received free screenings for sickle cell anemia. "We would go around in buses, and our medical coordinator would check the Black kids, give them physicals," Melvin said. There was also a BPP branch in nearby Tacoma.

"The presence of the [BPP] that was ready to put their life on the line for the Black community and the people knowing that was very inspirational," Melvin said. "I had the opportunity to be out there every day, circulating the paper, doing this and that, talking to the local businesses, taking donations, and it was always upbeat. There was always some incident, police brutality, where people were calling us, and we would go and stand security all night long. I think it was very inspirational for people to know that there was an organization to go to when they felt they were treated unjustly by police or . . . exploited by oppression. They felt like we could do something. And we would. We would do whatever we could."

The Seattle BPP chapter's work brought intensive police surveillance, Melvin recalled. "The police knew all of us by first name. If you was walking down the street and the police passed by, they'd say, 'Hey, what do you know about last night's this and that?' They would call on the phone and harass you all night long while you were standing security, call you all sorts of names. That was the kind of thing you put up with."

In 1972, the BPP Central Committee began to close party chapters around the country, directing its members to come to Oakland to work on the local election campaigns of Bobby Seale for mayor and *Black Panther* newspaper editor Elaine Brown for Oakland City Council. "There was some mobilization going on in Oakland around the survival programs," Melvin said. "We were moving out of the armed struggle, you know, sandbags and leather jackets, the whole military, paramilitary mentality. Huey was calling for the return to the original Black Panther Party and also the idea of participating in Black politics. In the beginning, the emphasis was the armed struggle, and we kind of got preoccupied with that mentality. I agreed with Huey about that."

However, Melvin said that moving BPP members from their local chapters to Oakland was "a bad move," a decision that ultimately contributed to the party's decline as a national organization. In Seattle, the BPP chapter was self-sustaining, Melvin said. "It was tough, but we generated our own income." After Panthers started moving to Oakland, "The [local] chapters and their programs kind of fell down. Their presence in the communities just wasn't there. Making Oakland the base of operations, I think, that was a great flaw, a tactical flaw. . . . I think it's true that we should have had a base of operations but not just in Oakland. It should have been spread around. . . . The development and the training we were advancing in Oakland could have been going on in other areas of the country. We put all our eggs in one basket. We all came and settled [in Oakland], and we were easily isolated."

After returning to Oakland, Melvin did precinct work for the election campaigns of Bobby and Elaine, neither of whom was elected. "[Their campaigns] opened up opportunities for Blacks in local government, [but] it's going to take lots more than Black people voting to change conditions [for Black people]," Melvin said. After the elections, Melvin's assignments included working at a local bar and grill owned by a family member of Huey and at the Oakland Community School, the award-winning elementary school founded by the BPP.

In its early years, the BPP was influenced by socialist revolutions then taking place throughout the world that toppled centuries of European colonial rule. Calling for a socialist revolution in the United States to end racism and oppression, the BPP adopted some of the principles of the various communist parties that sought to establish socialism in their countries. One of those principles was democratic centralism, whereby local Communist Party members elected their national leaders (sometimes called the Central Committee), which in turn ran the national parties and dictated policies to the membership.

In the BPP's system of democratic centralism, chapter coordinators or leaders were either elected locally or appointed by the party's national leadership body, the Central Committee. "When you join an organization, you submit to the centralism," Melvin said. "You identify with the goals, and you submit . . . full time. When you put yourself in that kind of situation, it is naturally going to change your whole attitude and the behavior you were doing before you got to the organization. And I don't see nothing wrong with that if a person wants to do that." However, he added, democratic centralism as implemented in the BPP "wasn't the best" because there was a lack of education about how to properly use it. Consequently, some Panthers in leadership positions developed "a personal attachment to [having] this power over somebody else. I think lots of mistakes were made. Lots of people abused it, and lots of people were misused," Melvin said.

Reflecting on the contributions of the Black Power movement, Melvin said that it helped Black people feel better about themselves. "I think that was very therapeutic in the sense that it got us out of the mode of accepting racism. You could fight it. You might not have planned it out, but you just fought it." On a personal level, he said, "[The movement changed] my life. I'm from the South. I was out to show that I was not a second-class citizen. It made me challenge myself, learn more, try to gain more skills and [do] all the other things I might [otherwise] not have done."

As for the lessons that young people can learn from the activists and groups of the Black Power era, Melvin said: "If [young people] investigate, they would see that we were living in a whole different situation at that time. . . . There were manufacturing jobs back in the sixties. The economic situation was not as devastating as it is today even though there was racism and inequality. . . . Some very significant changes are taking place both in this country and globally. . . . If [young people] study, I think they would recognize the need for an organization that would be far more advanced than the Black Panther Party ever was."

In 1965, at the start of the Black Power era, Black students were organizing against racism at Arlington State University (now the University of Texas at Arlington). One of their leaders was freshman Fred Bell (a.k.a. Fahim Minkah), a twenty-six-year-old air force veteran. Born in East Texas in 1939, Fred spent part of his childhood in Phoenix, where his father worked for several years. In the mid-1950s the Bell family moved back to Dallas, where Fred completed high school. Returning to the segregated society of Texas after living for several years in the more integrated society of Arizona was difficult for Fred, he said.

"I never adjusted myself to Jim Crow. I was always in conflict with Jim Crow laws," Fred said. "There was no Jim Crow for Blacks in Arizona. There was for Native Americans. I came back to Texas with a very hostile attitude of what I was going to do when faced with [racist] situations. I wanted to get out of the South because I had almost gotten killed by a constable. He was going to shoot me." To escape from racism, Fred joined the air force after graduating from high school. At the Illinois base where he was stationed, he discovered that the military was not immune to racism. After a year, he left the air force.

Back in Dallas, Fred heard about a group of civil rights activists who were picketing a cafeteria that refused to serve Blacks. Even though he understood the value of what the civil rights activists were doing, he said, Fred did not take part in the protest because the activists had pledged to remain nonviolent if they were physically attacked. "I didn't want to take part in that because I just felt like if they didn't want to serve me, if they didn't want to give me any respect, I didn't want them to have my money. I said, 'If I'm attacked, I'm going to fight.' I gave moral support to the civil rights movement. I guess I was radicalized already by circumstances and the things I had seen in my life." Fred would use this radicalism as a student.

He won a track scholarship to Arlington State University, where he was the only Black member of the track team. During his freshman year, he led some forty Black students on campus to protest the flying of the Confederate flag. The following year, Fred continued his campaign, meeting with the university's president, who was "receptive" to Fred's complaint. All the Black students signed a petition that Fred wrote. It stated that the symbolism of the Confederate flag was offensive to Blacks. He took the issue to the student congress, which ultimately asked the administration to remove the Confederate flag from campus. The university's alumni association contributed several thousand dollars for the repeal of the student congress's decision, which was nonbinding on the administration. Fred's leadership of the campaign to remove the Confederate flag from campus brought threats against his life. For self-defense he had a handgun that he concealed in a book. "I bought an English reader and cut out a hundred pages," he said.

When he started college, Fred wanted to be an aircraft engineer. "[But] I changed to pre-law because I was very interested in what happened in the Reconstruction era, the laws that were passed [then] that were still on the books." In one of his classes, he said, it was departmental policy to study the good points of slavery "to satisfy some of the feelings of the white kids." The only Black student in the class, Fred said he questioned the professor about why the negative issues regarding slavery were not discussed more. "He wouldn't answer. He would say, 'Read such and such.' I would write it down, go to the library, and usually got enough out of it to back up what I had said in class." After class, Fred would tell the professor, "What you gave me to read agreed with what I said, so why don't you stand up and agree with me in class? [The professor] said he couldn't for fear of losing his job."

During his sophomore year in college, 1966–1967, Fred worked full time at night and took classes during the day. It was around this time that he met members of the Dallas chapter of SNCC, whose founder, Ernest (Ernie) McMillan, had dropped out of Morehouse College to become a full-time SNCC organizer. At the time, SNCC was urging the Black community in Dallas to "rise up and retaliate against the unjustified deaths" of people killed by police, Fred recalled. Between going to school and working, Fred said, he would go to a place called the SNCC House. "I saw all these strange-looking people with big Afros. I started growing me a beard. I was there [reading their books], looking and observing. They talked basically the kind of language that I identified with, fighting back and challenging racist authorities."

After joining SNCC, Fred got involved in the group's protests at the OK chain of supermarkets. "We needed to do something to demonstrate the economic power of [Black] people in these neighborhood stores that were disrespectful to the people. The food was bad, the prices were high. We had a plan to take over all the retail outlets in Black neighborhoods to turn them into Black businesses to get more money circulating in the black community. OK supermarkets was the thing to come to people's minds. It wasn't too big but big enough to be significant."

SNCC members and their supporters targeted two OK supermarkets for their protests, Fred said, where they went and filled up their shopping carts. When they came to the counter to pay, they said they only wanted to buy one item. Explaining why they did this, Fred said: "This would cause the store owners a lot of trouble because they had to pay people to stay overtime and put stuff back on the shelves." After one SNCC protest at an OK supermarket in 1968, Fred, Ernie McMillan, and Matthew Johnson, leaders of the Dallas SNCC, were arrested. Charges against Fred were subsequently dropped because staff at the supermarket did not know if he had been inside the store. McMillan and Johnson, whom staff said were inside the store, were convicted for the destruction of private property and each sentenced to ten years in prison.

After McMillan and Johnson were convicted, Fred became chairman of the Dallas SNCC chapter, which started a community-wide boycott of the OK supermarket chain. On the day the boycott started, Fred recalled, "We gave them an orientation, got their names and phone numbers, [and] gave them some guidelines and some leaflets and a place to call us if something went wrong." SNCC members and supporters went to three or four of the chain's stores in the late afternoon, a busy shopping time, and passed out flyers urging shoppers to boycott OK. "We were amazed at how the Black community cooperated with us. [The boycott] was very effective," Fred said. Ultimately, the owners of the supermarket chain sold their stores to a group of Black businesspeople.

As noted, SNCC and its leaders were targeted for destruction by the FBI counterintelligence program in 1967. Unknown to Dallas members of SNCC, the organization began "dying around the country," Fred said. In 1968 he and fellow SNCC member Charles Beasley were among several people arrested for robbing a bank. "That bank robbery was a setup," Fred said. Prior to the robbery, he had loaned a shotgun to a male friend who, unknown to Fred, used the gun to burglarize a store. Fred later found out that his friend, while in jail for the burglary, was questioned by the FBI. On parole at the time on a previous conviction and seeking to keep from being indicted on the new charge, the friend agreed to help the FBI "get something" on Fred. Employing a COINTELPRO tactic commonly used by the FBI against the Black liberation movement around the country, Fred's friend "always suggested doing some crazy thing that was criminal," Fred recalled. "I kept saying that had nothing to do with the struggle, so I didn't take him up on it." Ignoring warnings from a family member that his friend was "a thief and a crook," Fred let the man use his car and stay at his apartment. There he planted articles connected to the robbery, Fred said.

To avoid a twenty-five-year sentence, Fred said he followed the advice of his attorneys and pleaded guilty to the bank robbery. He was sentenced to six years and placed in solitary confinement. "If I had known better, there's no way I would have pleaded guilty," he said. A few months after he was incarcerated, Fred filed a motion to have his sentence reduced. Meanwhile, he contracted a bad infection and "got real sick." Family members told a judge about his illness, and Fred was able to have an operation to get rid of the infection. "I could have sued them. I almost died in jail," he said. His motion to reduce his sentence was subsequently granted, and Fred was released after serving twenty-four months of his sentence.

By the time Fred got out of jail, the Dallas chapter of SNCC had been virtually destroyed due to the arrests and incarceration of its leaders and many of its members. In 1970, some former SNCC members and members of the Black Student Union at El Centro College received permission from the BPP Central Committee to form a National Committee to Combat Fascism/Dallas BPP chapter. Fred said that he did not trust some of the people in the new Dallas Panther chapter, so he did not join the group, which the BPP Central Committee expelled in 1972 after it was discovered that FBI informants had infiltrated the chapter. Fred created a program called Stop and Watch, modeled after the BPP's community patrols of the police. He explained: "If you saw a policeman stop someone in your neighborhood, stop at a certain distance and observe his activities. If you have a tape recorder, so much the better. If you have a camera with no film in it, make it look like you have film in it. Be careful not to behave in such a way the officer thinks it is a weapon. In a particular neighborhood where we first tested it out, the police didn't really stop people unless they really needed to stop them."

His renewed activism brought "a lot of heat" to get Fred back in prison for the bank robbery. He was tried and convicted on a different set of charges connected to the robbery ("a compromise verdict") and sentenced to ten years in federal prison. Fred had significant community support, and a defense fund was created for his case. Nevertheless, a federal judge refused to give the former Dallas SNCC chairman a bond so that he could stay out of prison while appealing his conviction, claiming that Fred was "too dangerous." He was sent to Leavenworth Federal Prison in Kansas, some six hundred miles from Dallas.

At Leavenworth, Fred worked in the prison factory and belonged to a group of Black activist prisoners who "converted themselves" from their criminal pasts. "Everybody wanted to be considered a political prisoner, a revolutionary," Fred said. In the final analysis, Fred said, going to prison may have saved his life. Otherwise, he might have sought retaliation for the destruction of the Dallas SNCC chapter. "[Retaliation] would have been incorrect," he said. After being released from prison on his second bank robbery conviction, Fred returned to Dallas, and in 1974, with Marvin Crenshaw, started a new Panther chapter in Dallas.

As in Dallas, during the Black Power era young Black activists in Houston were attempting to organize the Black community. One of those activists was Charles (a.k.a. Boko) Freeman. Born in 1951, Charles grew up in the Sunnyside community of Houston. "I got disenchanted with the school system and started cutting classes and playing hooky. I think most youth at that time were looking for some means of escape." Eventually Charles dropped out of high school.

Deciding that he needed "a change of environment," around 1967 Charles moved to New York City, where he enrolled in Andrew Jackson High School in Queens. "The first day I went to school there it was a shock to me because this was the first time I saw an integrated school," Charles said. "We had all nationalities. I had never experienced that in my years in Houston because everything there was pretty Black. We didn't have any integrated schools." Adding to his dismay, students at Andrew Jackson were having a demonstration on the first day of school. "A lot of kids were protesting and marching around in front of the school campus. They hung an effigy of the principal and the vice principal, who was Black, and then they burned [the effigies]." This was his "first contact with some type of resistance," Charles would recall. "Actually, that's where I became politicized and to understand what was taking place politically and socially in the society. I got a new awareness."

His new awareness included learning about Malcolm X, who had been assassinated in Harlem in 1965. "In Houston, you heard nothing about Malcolm X," Charles said. He bought "all kinds of paraphernalia" pertaining to Malcolm and listened to record albums with speeches of the slain ex–Nation of Islam national spokesman. "I figured at that point I wanted to make some kind of contribution to the [Black] plight." He joined Jackson High School's Black Student Union, which he saw as "an extension of what Malcolm X was about." Charles's work with the BSU eventually led him to become a community worker in the Queens branch of the Black Panther Party, helping to distribute the party's newspaper. "Most of the members in the party looked at themselves as the children of Malcolm X, so [the party] was an extension of his philosophy, particularly self-defense. I did admire the [BPP] social programs that were implemented," Charles said.

In school, Charles made the honor roll, something he never did in high school in Houston. "[But] I didn't see where it was necessary for me to finish [high school]. I looked at some of my friends who had actually finished in Houston, and they were in their earlier stages [of college]. They were working in concessions and stuff, selling popcorn and peanuts. The type of work they were doing was very menial. . . . A diploma was worth no more than toilet paper because there was nothing you could do with it as a Black person." Deciding that he wanted to do community work full time, Charles left Queens and returned to Houston with the intention of bringing the BPP to his hometown.

After returning home, Charles met twenty-one-year-old Carl Hampton, who was organizing People's Party II, a group modeled after the BPP. At the time, the FBI's COINTELPRO campaign against the BPP was at its height, and the party's national leadership had suspended approval of new chapters, but Carl was determined to organize the Black community in Houston. "He figured, why don't we just change the name? Call it People's Party II," Charles said, adding that the group was in essence an unrecognized chapter of the BPP. Charles said that he was the third person Carl recruited to People's Party II.

In June 1970 the fledgling group opened a community center in a "very notorious" part of Houston known for drugs, prostitution, and other crimes, Charles said. The first major activity of the center was to gather donations for a free clothing program. Political education classes were also held. One day in July, Charles said, some Houston police officers harassed a member of People's Party II who was selling the *Black Panther* newspaper in front of the community center, where Charles was inside at the time. During the police harassment, Carl and another brother drove up in front of the community center. Charles said that Carl, who was a passenger in the car, had a .45 pistol strapped to his shoulder.

"He had a legal reason to have the gun. He was transporting money from one facility to another one selling [BPP] newspapers," Charles said. Carl got out of the car and asked the police officer what was going on, Charles said. "[The police] saw him. That was something new in Houston, a brother with a .45 gun strapped on him. The police questioned Carl about what he was doing with his gun. He was very knowledgeable about the law, knowing that he had a right to bear arms. [The police] didn't want to hear that. They thought he was an uppity nigger. They [had] big red necks, and you could see them sweating. The officer in the car radioed for backup," Charles said. At that point, Charles and two other People's Party II members came out of the community center. "Us three were out there on the sidewalk. The police officer went for his gun, and Carl went for his. We already had ours, so it ended up being a standoff. Carl directed us to go back into the community center. We backed up into the center. There was no exchange of gunfire."

Thus began the first day of a ten-day armed standoff between People's Party II and Houston police, who surrounded the community center and sealed off the streets around it. "A couple of helicopters were flying around the building, and you could see the police running behind cars and stuff. They had full riot gear," Charles said. "Two white cops asked us to surrender, and Carl told them, 'We're not going to surrender.'" Prior to this confrontation, some Houston police officers had stomped a young Black man to death at a police station. "Carl didn't want to surrender himself. He figured he would take his chances dying on the street. He took a very heroic stand. You didn't see him flinch one time," Charles said.

There was an outpouring of community support, Charles said, recalling one occasion when people riding on a bus that was unable to get through the streets due to the police blockade got off the bus and held a rally in front of the community center. "That's what saved us [that day]," Charles said. On July 26, 1970, Carl Hampton died in a hail of bullets fired by a police sniper on the rooftop of a nearby church. Charles said that he was inside the community center when he learned that Carl had been shot and that it wasn't until later that night that he learned the People's Party II leader was dead. "Carl was singled out to be assassinated," Charles said. "He was a very dynamic brother who greatly influenced me because of the courageous stance that he took [against the police]."

In the hours following Carl's assassination, "busloads of people" were arrested, some who were supporters of People's Party II and others who lived in the neighborhood, Charles said. He avoided arrest by hiding out in the neighborhood. Subsequently, James Aaron was elected the chairman of People's Party II, which later became the Houston chapter of the BPP. The chapter operated such free community programs as food giveaways, breakfast for schoolchildren, busing to prisons, and a health clinic. After a neighborhood church donated space for the breakfast program, they started getting community support, Charles said.

Meanwhile, he and other Houston Panthers were frequently arrested and framed on various charges. "It was like a revolving door, but I didn't spend any big time" in jail, Charles said. One day he was arrested in front of the community center, and a police officer planted some marijuana in the pocket of his jacket, he said. Refusing to take a plea bargain, he went on trial and was acquitted by an all-white jury. "The police officers didn't rehearse their stories, so they came up with different versions [of the arrest], and it was obvious it was a setup," Charles said.

Following the decision of the BPP Central Committee to disband local chapters of the party and make Oakland the party's base of operations, Charles and other Houston Panthers moved to Oakland in 1974.

Reflecting on the contributions of the BPP, Charles said

its greatest strength was its community service programs, "feeding hungry kids, [and] helping the elderly not to get mugged." One of its greatest weaknesses was that many members, including himself, Charles said, focused too much on the party's leaders. "The organization centered around a personality [Huey Newton] . . . I think that contributed to the party's fall."

Another problem was that the way the BPP was organized prevented its members from having personal lives, Charles said. "[The party] was a paramilitary organization, and as a result we lived the lifestyle that was always bordering on warfare. You always kept . . . in tune as to what was going on around you. You didn't have a life. It was all wrapped up in the party. . . . The vision I held that captivated me [was] that we would actually rise up . . . and bring about change in other parts of the world. . . . I was very young, and I had no responsibilities other than myself." Echoing the sentiments of fellow Panther Melvin Dickson, Charles said, "In essence you give up personal goals and ambitions. You surrender yourself to the group. In essence that's what I did."

To Charles, mistakes that the party made were part of a process of growth. "Nobody came here being a professional . . . revolutionary, an activist to bring about social change." Young people, he said, can learn from the BPP. "If we want to make some kind of change or contribute something, whatever it is, we should go in and start work on it and do it. . . . A lot of the time [the BPP] would go to the media and talk about what we're going to do, and then the enemy had prior knowledge to counteract what we wanted to do. And they were very successful at it. That's what the whole [FBI counterintelligence program] was about. They can't be a step ahead unless you tell them about it." Charles said, "I'll always be a Panther." However, he doesn't believe there will ever be another organization like the BPP. "People say that history repeats itself, but I don't think this particular phenomenon of the Panther Party will ever repeat itself again as it existed then."

People's Party II was not the only group that attempted to establish a BPP chapter in Houston. According to Gwen Johnson (a.k.a. Ayanna Ade), who was a student at the University of Houston in the early 1970s, Bobby Seale once visited the campus at the request of the university's Organization of Black Student Unity (OBSU). Gwen was a member of the group, which wanted permission to set up a Panther chapter in Houston.

"The whole Free Huey movement was going on, and Bobby came to organize some money for the movement. [The OBSU] served as his security. There was some speculation that one guy who wasn't a part of our group but who contacted the party might have been an undercover agent. So, people in [the OBSU] backed off [from starting a BPP chapter]. The party got wind of that and backed off too," Gwen said.

The second of three children, Gwen was born in Houston in 1951. Her mother was a domestic worker, and her father was a truck driver who had a bachelor's degree in biology from Texas Southern University (TSU). While in high school, Gwen met members of the Nation of Islam. "I was always amazed at how beautiful they looked. I can remember my family saying, 'No, you don't want to be with them 'cause they preach hate.' [My family] never told me what that meant. All I knew was that they looked different than the other brothers and sisters in the community. There was always a mystique about them." Gwen's parents were religious, and her "day-to-day existence" primarily consisted of going to the Baptist church to which she and her family belonged. "I was greatly influenced through that," she said.

After graduating from high school in 1968, Gwen visited an aunt in Los Angeles. "I remember going to a festival in a park with all these Black folks. It just blew me away. Every time the park opened, I would be the first one to go into the parking lot. I would hang out all day and night. It was amazing. . . . I was kind of like a sponge absorbing everything." On the last night of the festival, "all hell broke loose" after a police officer and a Black woman in the crowd got into an argument, Gwen said. "I remember the cop saying something to the sister, and she told the cop she wasn't going to allow him to disrespect her. He slapped her. Cops were coming out of the bushes and the trees. Each cop had a shotgun. I can remember people running and screaming. . . . [I was excited] being with all the Black people and so many positive things they were talking about. Then to see [the cop slapping the Black woman], it was mind-boggling."

While in Los Angeles, Gwen went to a community rally, where for the first time she saw members of the Black Panther Party. "These brothers and sisters were standing tall and marching strong. I wanted to know who they were," Gwen said. One of the speakers at the meeting was Alprentice "Bunchy" Carter, the founder and leader of the Southern California BPP chapter. "When I heard Bunchy, I was totally blown away." After the rally, Gwen said she "de-permed" her hair. "I got a natural. It was kind of like I was on a mission from that day forward."

After returning to Houston, Gwen enrolled at TSU. "I started seeking anything and anybody to share information with me. I was always searching and looking." Before she became a student there, two Black students were arrested for killing a police officer on the TSU campus. When Gwen started her freshman year at TSU, the trial of the two students was underway in a small town about one hundred miles from Houston. Buses left from campus to take students to the trial. Despite her parents' disapproval, Gwen said that "without fail, if the buses were going," she went to the trial. "Going to the trial seemed to help raise my consciousness," she said. As noted, Gwen was active in the Organization of Black Student Unity at the University of Houston, to which she transferred from Texas Southern. The OBSU adopted the philosophy of the BPP and had a free breakfast program modeled after that of the Panthers' program. "I would cook up the food and have the tables ready by the time that the kids came in to get their meals," Gwen said. "We also had a Saturday school. I really loved it." Years later, when those kids had become adults, some of those who participated would share their memories about it with her. "[They] would walk up to me and say how the breakfast program and the Saturday school had such an influence on their lives," Gwen said.

After she left the OBSU, Gwen started working with some of the people who were in People's Party II. "They kind of knew me because of my involvement with [the] free breakfast program, and so they approached me," Gwen said. Charles Freeman and James Aaron of People's Party II were organizing a clothing program. "I had done that type of work before," Gwen said, and Charles and James asked for her help. Eventually she started working full time with People's Party II as it evolved into the Houston chapter of the BPP.

In the BPP, Gwen was a single parent with two young

sons. "It truly never felt like I was a single parent. I always had a strong sense of family when I was in the party. It felt like my children had lots of mommies and lots of fathers." But it wasn't easy, she said. "I can remember sometimes being so tired I couldn't keep my eyes open. Sometimes I was pissed off at the things I had to do [in the party], and I didn't want to do them. But, overall, the work I was doing was positive. I had a sense of purpose, that I was getting something accomplished."

When members of the Houston Panthers began relocating to Oakland, Gwen was pregnant with her second son. "I didn't come [to Oakland] right away. As a matter of fact, there was a murkiness right around that time. It was like, well, she didn't come to Oakland. Is she really a member of the party? Should we let her come?" At the time, the BPP needed more teachers at the alternative elementary school it ran, Oakland Community School. Gwen said she had dropped out of college nine credit hours short of graduation in order to work full time with the Houston BPP. Party officials in Oakland encouraged her to get her college degree. "I went back and graduated, with the understanding that I would come (to Oakland) to teach," she said. When she was able to travel with her new baby, Gwen came to Oakland in 1974. At Oakland Community School, she did "a little bit of everything," including teaching English and for a while coordinating the school's math program.

When Gwen joined the BPP, she said, "I had wanted to go to medical school and was told that eventually the party would send me, after we don't have this campaign going on, when we don't have this work going on. It never materialized." Eventually, along with some other Panthers, Gwen said she submitted a document to the BPP leadership requesting changes in the way the party operated. "It [the document] was never intended to antagonize. It was done out of love," Gwen said. Dissatisfied with the BPP leadership's response to their requests, many of the Panthers who called for changes left the group. Gwen was among them. "I loved my comrades. It was really hard for me to leave. It was very painful for a long time. I was so totally alone and isolated. . . . There is a sociological connection when you work in an organization for any length of time, and you give your mind, soul, and your body. . . . [The party] was such a closed society. It didn't afford us the opportunity to grow and develop socially. . . . [Gwen and some other Panthers] wanted to be involved with the people of the community, to go back to school, to develop our skills. If we were involved in every aspect of the community, we couldn't help but grow stronger."

Gwen became part of "the Family," a support group made up of other former Panthers in Oakland. "We knew that we needed each other. We needed a strong support system. Most of us weren't originally from Oakland. We had children, so we made sure all of the children were taken care of." Most BPP members lived together, but members of the Family did not, Gwen said. "We all had our own individual homes, but we interacted quite a lot for the first couple of years after I left [the party]." She later returned home to Houston.

"Blown away" by all the skills she learned in the BPP, Gwen said that being a Panther was one of the most positive periods in her life. "One thing I learned was that we can do anything. I don't see the sky as being the limit. There is nothing worth having if you're not willing to work for it. Perseverance is what we have to be about. . . . If we truly are going to bring about change, we have to figure out how to institutionalize those things we do well. If we can't, [we're] doomed to fail."

Like Gwen Johnson, Tondalela Woolfolk's first encounter with the BPP occurred at a political rally in Los Angeles, where she had just moved from her hometown, Chicago. Born in 1950, Tondalela was the second of eight children and grew up in a Catholic family who lived in a housing project on Chicago's West Side. Her Georgia-born father, a laborer, was a former member of the US Coast Guard. Tondalela's mother grew up in West Virginia before moving to Chicago.

"My father was an introvert," Tondalela recalled. "He didn't want anyone from the outside in [our house], and he really didn't want us to go out. He monitored our every movement." Nevertheless, she said, she loved her father. "[I] wanted to do everything to please him."

In contrast, Tondalela said, her mother was "outside of the house a great deal." She was the chair of the PTA at the school that Tondalela and her siblings attended and a member of the board of the boys' club. "My father didn't like that," Tondalela explained.

Her parents separated, and her father went back to Georgia when Tondalela was still young. "I didn't like my mother being a single parent," Tondalela recalled. "I was always expected to help around the house, but then I became responsible for meals and more responsible for my brothers and sisters and their appearance."

To give Tondalela more time for herself, her mother convinced a high school counselor to let Tondalela live at the school's convent for a while.

The Woolfolk siblings attended Catholic schools in Chicago. In the neighborhood where they lived, Tondalela became friends with some Black gang members. She joined some of them to start a Black Action Council at Providence High School. One of the nuns at the school chose Tondalela to participate in an Upward Bound program that had a study group. That's where she first heard about Black Power and Marxism-Leninism.

Tondalela's political activism grew when she joined the Ecumenical Institute, a West Side Chicago organization. The institute was run by a group of white Protestant ministers and lay people, whose mission was to improve the cultural, economic, and political conditions in the West Side Black community. The institute received federal antipoverty funds. Tondalela became active in the High School House, one of the institute's programs.

"It was a residential setting that was half white and half Black," Tondalela said. "We were teenagers. We were trained how to be change agents."

High School House students created a ten-year plan for world social change. When the staff refused to hear the plan, the students took over a staff meeting. This "insurrection" led to the demise of High School House, Tondalela said.

She was asked to leave Providence High School during her junior year because of insubordination to a nun who was her English teacher. "I had a smart mouth and had developed into something of a rebel. I don't remember how the confrontation started, but . . . I refused to apologize and was put out of the classroom."

Leaving Providence High School in 1966, sixteen-year-old Tondalela went to Riverside, California, to live with a white, middle-class family of a High School House member. Her host family took her to a political rally, where Black Panther Party members were speaking. Remembering the rally, Tondalela said, "They were real Black and big. They had a lot of pride about them. You got a real sense of seriousness. I found that to be exciting because white people were afraid of them. That interested me quite a bit."

In Riverside, Tondalela had her first experience being a Black student at a predominantly white school. She described Riverside Polytechnic High School as "'*Leave It to Beaver* Land,' seeing white people in their own setting." In Chicago, the white people with whom Tondalela had contact said they were working to fight racism. "Most of the white people I was running into at Riverside were acknowledged racists and didn't give a damn whether you knew it. It was very traumatic and very painful."

Tondalela had always been a good student and had never heard of a tracking system until she attended high school in Riverside. In this system, she said, "Minority students were placed in less-challenging academic courses." In her honors English course, Tondalela never earned a grade above C.

Tondalela left Riverside in June 1968 after experiencing more than racism at school. "I would not stand during the 'Star Spangled Banner,'" she said, "and I refused to say the Pledge of Allegiance. I didn't think those things had anything to do with me and that they were hypocritical."

After leaving Riverside, Tondalela went to New Haven, Connecticut, where some adults she knew persuaded her to join a program for inner-city high school students at Yale University. There were about seventy-five Black, Latino, and Native American youth from all over the country who were students in the program.

"Yale was part of a conspiracy to co-opt young political leaders and take them off the streets that summer [1968]," Tondalela said. "There was a Black Power movement going on right there on campus. . . . They were pushing everyone to make changes from within."

At Yale, she became friends with a young woman who was the local contact for the Black Panther Party. Her friend introduced Tondalela to Ericka Huggins, who was newly widowed and had a baby girl. She and her late husband John had been members of the BPP chapter in Los Angeles, where John was second in command. Tondalela met Ericka not long after John, a New Haven native, and Alprentice "Bunchy" Carter, the leader of the BPP chapter in Los Angeles, were shot to death in January 1969 by members of United Slaves, the Black-nationalist cultural group, at a meeting of Black students at the University of California-Los Angeles.

Impressed by Ericka Huggins's thoughtfulness and how she talked about "repression and the economic and political roots of the oppression of Black people," Tondalela decided to join the BPP. Ericka was in the early stages of organizing the BPP in New Haven, so Tondalela went to New York City where the party was already established. At the BPP office in Harlem in May 1969, she was assigned to the Ministry of Information cadre and sold BPP newspapers. "I was pretty good verbally, and I would sell my papers in about two-and-a-half hours."

Tondalela discovered that growing up in a large poor family in Chicago housing projects was better than living in the Bronx "tenement slum" where she lived in New York City. "I wasn't real excited about the living conditions."

She lived with an older Panther comrade sister, "B," and her three children. To bring income into their house, the two women worked as state food inspectors. Their jobs enabled them to get food and supplies for the BPP's free breakfast program. It was very gratifying, Tondalela said, to go into a grocery store and threaten them with a boycott if they didn't donate to the breakfast program.

While coping with substandard living conditions, Tondalela also had to contend with the "free love" sexual relations between BPP women and men. During the 1960s and 1970s, many American youth had sex with multiple sexual partners as part of a "free love" ethos. Tondalela said, "Everybody [in the BPP in New York] was screwing everybody. The brothers tried to put pressure on the sisters, saying that this was something they were required to do. . . . The whole sex thing in the party was a little out of hand."

B was older than Tondalela and insisted that Panther women had to be respected. BPP representatives from headquarters in Oakland came to New York, Tondalela said, to "kind of straighten that out."

In April 1969, a few weeks before Tondalela's arrival in Harlem, twenty-one members of the BPP in New York City were indicted on charges of conspiring to bomb and make long-range rifle attacks on two police stations and an education office. The party had to organize tremendous financial and legal resources to defend the New York 21, as the defendants came to be called.

Following their arrest, police harassment of the New York BPP escalated. The police raided the BPP office in Jamaica, New York. Afterward, a Panther brother was assigned to temporarily stay with Tondalela, B, and her children in the apartment where they lived. On one occasion, several Panthers were in the apartment.

"Some brothers doing security had walkie-talkies outside," Tondalela recalled. "Everybody was afraid because of what had happened to the Jamaica [BPP] branch. . . . We heard gunshots through the walkie-talkie, and I went off. I got behind the sofa."

The police were preparing to surround the building, Tondalela said. "There were cars of pigs driving real slow by our building loaded down [with] so much hardware. It was getting real intense." Several party members in the apartment started arguing. Tondalela recalled, "[I was] upset that people would argue and have weapons while we were potentially under siege."

Ultimately the Panthers left the apartment without a confrontation with the police that day. "[But it scared] the shit out of me," Tondalela said. "I was sheltered growing up. I wasn't a gangbanger. I didn't know about getting shot at. . . . It was not my turf. . . . I'm going to dodge bullets where I know all the alleys and I know the people."

She left New York and went home to Chicago to join the Illinois chapter of the Black Panther Party, led by the charismatic twenty-one-year-old Fred Hampton. Several Chicago party members were Tondalela's former classmates at Providence High. "I knew who I could trust, who I would be under fire with," Tondalela said.

She found that the BPP chapter in her hometown was better organized and more disciplined than the New York BPP, whose leadership, Tondalela conceded, had "been kind of decimated" by the New York 21 case. Fred was a strong chairman who maintained tight discipline, she said. "[Fred] was always looking for this alertness. You had to be where you were supposed to be at a certain time doing what you were supposed to be doing. . . . He came down on [party members] like a ton of bricks if he found out they were using drugs."

Tondalela discovered that attitudes about sexual relations between Panther women and men were different in

Chicago than they were in New York. "Fred . . . had very definite ideas about a woman's role in the revolution. It had nothing to do with being prone," she said.

The free breakfast program and the free health clinic were two of the BPP's most successful programs in Chicago, Tondalela recalled. "[Fred's] emphasis was on building a movement that would tear the [political] structure down and put in another more humane, more equitable structure. His emphasis was on program-building." Fred organized a coalition of Black, white, and Hispanic youth gangs in the area, which Tondalela and others have described as the "original Rainbow Coalition."

The popularity of the BPP community survival programs and Fred Hampton's organization of gangs brought greater visibility to the Chicago Panthers. It also increased the FBI's scrutiny of the group. Fred's life was threatened several times, Tondalela recalled, and he was convinced that "any minute he was going to be offed." Tondalela and other Panther women in Chicago were sometimes assigned to provide security for Fred when he spoke at public events. Fred was concerned that there were "agent provocateurs and infiltrators" in the Illinois BPP chapter, Tondalela said. He called a meeting of the chapter and expelled the entire membership until further notice.

On November 13, 1969, Chicago Black Panther Spurgeon "Jake" Winters and two Chicago police officers were killed during a shootout. Less than a week later, according to FBI records, Fred's name was added to the "Rabble Rouser Index," a list of people the FBI claimed "demonstrated a potential for fomenting racial discord."

On the morning of December 4, Chicago BPP members awoke to the news that Fred Hampton and Mark Clark, the leader of the BPP in Peoria, Illinois, had been shot to death by Chicago police officers in a predawn raid. To Tondalela, Fred's death was immense. "[It was] the loss of the organization that I had devoted my life to . . . which meant that a great deal of my life was gone." Along with many other Black Panthers in Chicago, Tondalela left the BPP soon after Fred and Mark were killed.

Reflecting on her experiences, Tondalela noted the financial, legal, and political problems caused by the imprisonment of BPP cofounder Huey P. Newton for killing an Oakland police officer. "I didn't want to spend all my time keeping Huey out of jail. I didn't think that was the purpose of the struggle. At that point, I guess Huey was a legend. . . . I can imagine what prison can do. Huey was a casualty, and we should have treated him as such. I think it came from a lack of adequate self-criticism. At some point, Huey became a shell of the person who started the Black Panther Party."

Like many Black Power era groups, the BPP was influenced by revolutionary ideology and theory of struggles in other countries. Tondalela said that the party failed to critically analyze whether those ideologies and theories could be applied to the United States. "The most important lesson I learned was that you could not take a theory and apply it to a situation," Tondalela said. "That's not the way you did things. You did research to find out what the situation was, and you formed a hypothesis, and you tested it out. . . . So, your theory evolved from reality."

Epilogue

It is beyond the scope of this book to examine what led to the decline of the Black Power era. For a variety of reasons, not the least of which was the FBI's brutal COINTELPRO campaign to destroy the Black liberation movement, assisted by other law enforcement agencies, Black Power consciousness began to decline after 1975.

According to historian Peniel E. Joseph, Black Power was "a series of creative political and intellectual experiments that varied depending on political geography, social class, gender, and political ideology." In this regard, the Black Power era activists who were interviewed for this book provided a range of opinions about their experiences and the lessons they learned.

Former Black Panthers assessed their experiences in chapter 7. Other Black Power era activists also reflected on their work and experiences. Joyce Grant said that in Boston, Black activists continually argued over who was going to lead. Some leaders were people "who were getting their contracts from the city," she said. "They survived because of their close ties to the white power structure. They were not risk takers. You've got to protect the risk takers because they don't survive."

In the National Welfare Rights Organization, many leaders stayed on too long, Jackie Pope said. "We needed new infusions of blood. But this was their domain. This gave them legitimacy, and they liked the power and the publicity." Furthermore, when the woman who headed the Brooklyn NWRO went to work in the group's national office in Washington, DC, there was no one with her charisma to replace her, Jackie said. "That would say to me that you have to be mindful of what you do to an organization when you [remove] a charismatic person." Jackie added that her involvement in the welfare rights movement made her into a totally different person:

> I saw this country for what it really is. I began to look at the issue of poverty and poor people in a whole different light. I was no longer ashamed of getting public assistance. I think the weakness was that our mechanism for evaluating where we should go from [there] was less than strong. It was too little. It should have been more intensive. We were unclear of where we were going to take [the movement]. . . . Once [the welfare department] learned our tactics, learned our strategies, and was able to come back after reeling on the ropes, we didn't know what to do when people started dropping out.

Black Power era activists have failed to adequately document their history, said Lee Rose. "There is no library [of the Black Power era]," she said.

> Each time there is a movement, what happens in the past is hardly ever connected to what is happening

> now. There is no tie in the past that the children can go to, which says this is how it was. So, the kids have to start all over again from the beginning. [Black Power] was a movement in the entire country. . . . These were huge organizations. . . . If we are ever to learn anything from what we've done in the past and what we're going to do in the future, you have to have a mode of leaving something for these kids to look to. I am sad about what we didn't leave.

Joe Hicks also expressed concern about the lack of education that young people receive about the Black Power era. "I think we have to first of all gain control of our own history, interpret it properly and read it. We need our young people to be students of history, to read and be able to interpret history. Also, people of our generation need to be clear about putting [the history] out to young people and be willing to engage in struggle [with] young people." Commenting on his work in Los Angeles during the Black Power era, Joe said:

> What the Black Power movement did was make me quite convinced that my whole life will always be dedicated to social change and that, since 1965 when I walked out of my door looking for the first meeting of folks dealing with social change, I have not stopped. If this ain't working, then I'm looking for something that will work for me so that I don't become tied down and defend a particular type of formation or organization. The Black Power struggle gave me a certain sort of light in my soul that always keeps me looking for those kinds of avenues and organizational models and the

kinds of issues that will push us onward. It ain't over, not by a long shot.

One hotly debated issue during the Black Power era was whether Black activists working for social change in America should ally themselves with white activists. Mike Hamlin, Earl Rose, Lee Rose, and Tanya Russell were members of the Black Workers Congress, a Black Marxist group that worked with white activists in the labor movement. "I think this whole question of 'Can you go it alone?' is once again going to be a question tearing at the fabric, because we are not in it alone," Lee said. "I clearly believe that Black nationalism has a strong role to play in our education. But if you don't go beyond that, it turns in on itself and can eat you from the inside out. There is just no way nationalism is going to be an end to all of Black people's problems."

Mike, who cofounded the Black Workers Congress, the Dodge Revolutionary Union Movement, and the League of Revolutionary Black Workers, said that the latter two groups had "a profound impact" on Detroit's automobile industry. "We forced the unions to create a situation where Blacks could move up to top ranks of leadership. We forced the industry to hire more Black management people. . . . We recruited probably some of the best and brightest young people in the community that kind of transformed them from individuals to people who were caring and conscious about people in the community as a whole." On a personal level, Mike said, "[My activism] gave me a reason to live. I could fight, strike a blow, and advance our people. I was doing something about what I felt were unjust and terrible conditions."

Activists in the Ocean Hill–Brownsville movement for

community-controlled schools put up "a valiant struggle," said Rev. C. Herbert Oliver. "Though we did not gain [all of our goals], we set a pace. . . . What we were trying to achieve is what must be achieved. Blacks in the inner cities and all over the country must get a proper education. We did not have a political base. We had an ideological base, a common feeling that something needed to be done, but it was not on a political foundation. The United Federation of Teachers had a political base, and they used it to destroy us. Any program that is going to last has got to have a political base . . . otherwise it's a fleeting struggle."

"The personal is political" was a phrase popularized by an essay of the same name written by feminist Carol Hanisch in 1969. The phrase, used by feminist, Black Power, and student activists, declared that the individual lives and experiences of people cannot be separated from the structure of their society. Black Power era organizations should have paid more attention to the personal needs of their members, said Zakiya Somburu. "There was just too much of . . . 'the agenda, the agenda, the agenda.' We [Blacks] are a wounded people, and by and large all of the people that were involved wanted to support and politicize a wounded people. There wasn't any place for hurt, pain, and disappointment. So consequently, you get a lot of wounded people that had their own issues that weren't being addressed, and often times that got in the way and obstructed progress in what we wanted to do."

For Tanya Russell, "[Black Power] came along with one clear message: 'We're Black, and we love it.' There's no ambivalence about that." Tanya added: "Black Power helped me to like myself. . . . When I got involved in the Black Panther breakfast program, I wasn't a Panther. I didn't know the people in the room. I got off on just washing dishes because it was so invigorating just to be part of it. . . . What that period of time said to me was that it's real important that you're able to feel that love. For a short moment, Black Power reinforced that we can organize, we can plan. Black Power showed we can work together."

Notes

Preface

The quotes from Jewel Parker Rhodes are from her book *The African American Guide to Writing and Publishing Nonfiction* (Broadway Books, 2001).

The quote from Rhonda Y. Williams is from her essay "'We're Tired of Being Treated Like Dogs': Poor Women and Power Politics in Black Baltimore," in the Fall/Winter 2001 issue of *Black Scholar* magazine.

The quote from Robert L. Allen is from a letter he wrote to me in 1992.

The quotes from Kenneth Heineman are from his paper, "Giving Voice to the Voiceless? The Challenge of Interviewing Social Activists," presented at the 1995 Oral History Association conference in Milwaukee.

The quote from Sarah Lawrence-Lightfoot is from her book *I've Known Rivers: Lives of Loss and Liberation* (Addison-Wesley, 1994).

The quote from Peniel E. Joseph is from his essay "Black Liberation without Apology: Reconceptualizing the Black Power Movement," in the Fall/Winter 2001 issue of *Black Scholar* magazine.

Chapter 1

The quote by Malcolm X at the beginning of the chapter is taken from his April 1964 speech, "The Ballot or the Bullet." The speech may be found in its entirety in *Malcolm X Speaks*, edited by George Breitman.

"Fearless propagandist" is taken from John McCartney, *Black Power Ideologies: An Essay in African American Political*

Thought (Temple University Press, 2010). "A transitional figure in the continuum of Afro-American activism" and "a benchmark in the historical progression of Black protest thought," are taken from William L. Van Deburg, *New Day in Babylon: The Black Power Movement and American Culture, 1965–1975* (University of Chicago Press, 1992). For more about the impact of Malcolm X on the Black Power era, see Robert L. Allen, *Black Awakening in Capitalist America* (Doubleday, 1969).

The information about the Lowndes County Freedom Organization is taken from Clayborne Carson, *In Struggle: SNCC and the Black Awakening of the 1960s* (Harvard University Press, 1995) and from Herbert H. Haines, *Black Radicals and the Civil Rights Mainstream, 1954–1970* (University of Tennessee Press, 1988).

The information about the 1965 Watts rebellion is taken from Lerone Bennett Jr., *Before the Mayflower: A History of Black America*, 6th ed., 1987.

The quote by Congressman Powell is taken from www.blackhistory.com. Prior to Powell, among those who used the term "Black Power" were Marcus Garvey, Paul Robeson, and Richard Wright.

Throughout this book, Kwame Ture will be referred to by his birth name, Stokely Carmichael, which he used during a major portion of the Black Power era.

The information about the "Mississippi March Against Fear" and SNCC's use of the slogan "Black Power" is taken from Carson, *In Struggle*.

The information about the Black Power Planning Conference is taken from Carson, *In Struggle*.

The quote referring to the Black Panther Party as "arguably the premier Black left organization of the African American liberation struggle," is taken from Charles E. Jones, ed., *The Black Panther Party [Reconsidered]* (Black Classic Press, 1998).

The information about the FBI counterintelligence program's campaign against "black nationalist hate groups" is taken from the 1976 Church Committee report: US Congress, Senate, Select Committee to Study Governmental Operations with Respect to Intelligence Activities, *Final Report*, 94th Congress, 2nd session, 1976, available at https://www.intelligence.senate.gov/sites/default/files/94755_II.pdf.

"Nobody missed them" and the information about the Black Power Conference is taken from Floyd B. Barbour, ed., *The Black Power Revolt* (P. Sargent, 1968).

The quote by August Wilson is from his essay "The Ground on Which I Stand," *American Theater*, September 1996.

Chapter 2

The quote at the beginning of the chapter is from a July 15, 1993, interview with Tanya Russell.

Quotes and statements by Hardy Frye are from a July 14, 1993, interview.

Quotes and statements by Joe Hicks are from a July 8, 1993, interview.

"'Us' Blacks as opposed to 'them' whites" comes from Scot Brown, "The US Organization, Black Power Vanguard Politics, and the United Front Ideal: Los Angeles and Beyond," *Black Scholar*, Fall/Winter 2001.

Quotes and statements by Rev. C. Herbert Oliver are from an August 14, 1993, interview.

The police officer who arrested Oliver was the infamous Eugene "Bull" Connor. Later, as commissioner of police, Connor used billy clubs and dogs to brutalize civil rights demonstrators during the successful campaign organized by Rev. Fred Shuttlesworth in the spring of 1963 to desegregate public facilities in Birmingham.

Quotes and statements by Joyce Grant are from an August 3, 1993, interview.

For an account of the movement for community-controlled schools in Boston, see Mel King, *Chain of Change, Struggles for Black Community Development* (South End Press, 1981).

Quotes and statements by Jacqueline (Jackie) Pope are from a July 15, 1993, interview.

The NWRO was not a Black Power group, per se. Its founder, George Wiley, a Black chemistry professor at Syracuse University, was the leader of the Syracuse chapter of CORE and later served briefly as the group's national associate director. Wiley disagreed with CORE's adoption of Black Power and left the organization in 1966. He subsequently founded NWRO, most of whose members and leaders were African American women. For more about NWRO, see Jacqueline Pope, *Biting the Hand That Feeds Them: Organizing Women on Welfare at the Grass Roots Level* (Praeger, 1989), and Guida West, *The National Welfare Rights Movement: The Social Protest of Poor Women* (Praeger, 1981).

Quotes and statements by Frances M. Beal are from a July 18, 1993, interview.

Quotes and statements by Joye Williams are from a September 24, 1993, interview.

Quotes and statements by Lee Rose are from an August 1, 1993, interview.

Quotes and statements by Earl Rose are from a July 31, 1993, interview.

Quotes and statements by Mike Hamlin are from an April 22, 1997, interview.

Quotes and statements by Antonio (Tony) Zamora are from a September 23, 1996, interview.

The Black Arts Movement is discussed in articles written by two of its major proponents: Larry Neal, "The Social Background of the Black Arts Movement," and Amiri Baraka (LeRoi Jones), "Black Art," both in *Black Scholar*, January 1987.

Quotes and statements by Zakiya Somburu are from a July 20, 1993, interview.

Quotes and statements by Robin (Che) Parker are from a May 16, 1994, interview.

Quotes and statements by Father Earl A. Neil are from an August 14, 1993, interview.

Quotes and statements by Tanya Russell are from the previously cited July 15, 1993, interview.

Chapter 3

Huey P. Newton, "Executive Mandate No. 1," was delivered May 2, 1967, and later published in a pamphlet: Huey P. Newton, *Essays from the Minister of Defense* (Black Panther Party, 1968).

Reference to the Hoover memo to FBI field offices is from the final Church Committee report.

The quotes by Emory Douglas originate from a March 1991 phone interview.

The report on the *Black Panther* by the Committee on Internal

Security of the House of Representatives, *The Black Panther Party, Its Origin and Development as Reflected in Its Official Weekly Newspaper, the "Black Panther Black Community News Service,"* was released on October 6, 1970.

The quotes from David DuBois ("I was no spring chicken" and "When I came to the Black Panther Party") were written in a letter from David to me.

Reference to the Los Angeles Police Department intelligence memo (On August 25, 1967 and "A Los Angeles Police Department") is from the final Church Committee report.

Chapter 4

Quotes and statements by Hardy Frye are from the previously cited July 14, 1993, interview.

Quotes and statements from Eva Partee McMillan are from a September 7, 1996, interview.

Quotes and statements by Rev. C. Herbert Oliver are from the previously cited August 14, 1993, interview.

Quotes and statements by Jackie Pope are from the previously cited August 15, 1993, interview.

Quotes and statements by Joyce Grant are from the previously cited August 3, 1993, interview.

Quotes and statements by Zakiya Somburu are from the previously cited July 20, 1993, interview.

Quotes and statements by Joye Williams are from the previously cited September 24, 1993, interview.

Quotes and statements by Tony Zamora are from the previously cited September 23, 1996, interview. Tony was my boss when I did a brief stint as a clerical worker at the Purdue University Black Cultural Center in the fall of 1973.

Quotes and statements by Mike Hamlin are from the previously cited April 27, 1997, interview.

"Lumpen" is a Marxist term referring to the chronically unemployed. According to a Church Committee report, at least one undercover informant infiltrated the first Black Panther Party chapter in Detroit.

Quotes and statements by Father Earl Neil are from the previously cited August 14, 1993, interview.

Chapter 5

For more about the attempted merger of SNCC and the BPP, see Clayborne Carson, *In Struggle: SNCC and the Black Awakening of the 1960s* (Harvard University Press, 1995), and *Revolutionary Suicide: The Autobiography of Huey P. Newton*, first published in 1973.

Quotes and statements by Hardy Frye are from the previously cited July 14, 1993, interview.

Quotes and statements by Mike Hamlin are from the previously cited April 27, 1997, interview.

Quotes and statements by Joe Hicks are from the previously cited July 8, 1993, interview.

Quotes and statements by Joyce Grant are from the previously cited August 3, 1993, interview.

Quotes and statements by Tanya Russell are from the previously cited July 15, 1993, interview.

Quotes and statements by Frances Beal are from the previously cited July 18, 1993, interview.

Quotes and statements by Lee Rose are from the previously cited August 1, 1993, interview; quotes and statements by Jackie Pope are from the previously cited August 15, 1993, interview.

Quotes and statements by Rev. C. Herbert Oliver are from the previously cited August 14, 1993, interview.

Quotes and statements by Earl Rose are from the previously cited July 31, 1993, interview.

Quotes and statements by Che Parker are from the previously cited May 16, 1994, interview.

Quotes and statements by Father Earl Neil are from the previously cited August 14, 1993, interview.

Chapter 6

My talk to a Black literature class took place at Western Michigan University on December 5, 1994.

The quote describing the aims of the BPP survival programs is taken from the Fall 1974 Supplement to the *Whole Earth Catalog*, published in *Co-Evolution Quarterly*.

The quote by Huey P. Newton ("We called them survival programs") is from *To Die for the People: The Writings of Huey P. Newton* (Random House, 1972).

Kit Kim Holder's 1990 doctoral dissertation (University of Massachusetts) is titled "The History of the Black Panther Party 1966–1972: A Curriculum Tool for Afrikan American Studies."

The quote by Bobby Seale is from *Seize the Time: The Story of the Black Panther Party and Huey P. Newton* (Random House, 1970).

The quote by Huey Newton about political action is from *To Die for the People.*

Information about the tactical disagreement among members of the BPP can be found in the 1976 Church Committee final report and in Huey Newton, "On the Defection of Eldridge Cleaver from the Black Panther Party and the Defection of the Black Panther Party from the Black Community," *Black Panther*, April 17, 1971.

The quote by Huey Newton about the relationship between politics and the material needs of the Black community is from *To Die for the People.*

Thomas Hobbes' book is *Leviathan Parts I and II.*

Philip S. Foner discusses the BPP's program against police brutality in his book *The Black Panthers Speak*, first published 1970.

For more information about the BPP's community patrols of the police, see Newton, *Revolutionary Suicide*, and Seale, *Seize the Time.* In April 1967 California legislator Donald Mulford introduced a bill to change a gun statute in California. This was designed to disarm the BPP and end its police-alert patrols. On May 2 Seale led a group of Panthers to the state capitol in Sacramento where he read the party's "Executive Mandate No. 1," a statement written by Huey, upholding the right of Black people to arm themselves against "terror, brutality, murder and repression" by "racist police agencies."

For a discussion of the Denzil Dowell case and the quotes about the community patrols of the police in Richmond, California, see Seale, *Seize the Time.*

See *The Whole Earth Catalog*, Fall 1974, for information about the safety of senior citizens in Oakland. The dates of the study's six-week period were August 21 to October 1, 1972.

For more details about the BPP's program for senior citizens, see *Black Panther,* December 16, 1972; April 21, May 15, and May 19, 1973; and January 26, 1975; Elaine Brown, *A Taste of Power: A Black Woman's Story* (first published 1992);

Roderick D. Bush, *The New Black Vote: Politics and Power in Four American Cities* (Synthesis, 1984). On April 17, 1973, in a field of four candidates, Bobby Seale forced the incumbent mayor of Oakland, John Reading, into a runoff election. Defeated by Reading on May 15, Bobby nevertheless won a respectable 40 percent of the vote. Elaine Brown lost her race for Oakland City Council but garnered over thirty-four thousand votes. The Seale-Brown campaign registered over thirty thousand new voters in Oakland, paving the way for the election of the city's first Black mayor, Lionel Wilson, in 1977.

For more information about the creation of the *Black Panther* newspaper, see chapter 3.

The quote from the editorial "Why Was Denzil Dowell Killed?" is from *Black Panther*, April 25, 1967.

The quote by Eldridge Cleaver is from the 1970 report by the US House of Representatives, Committee on Internal Security: *The Black Panther Party: Its Origin and Development as Reflected in Its Official Weekly Newspaper, the "Black Panther Black Community News* Service."

See Newton, *Revolutionary Suicide*, for a discussion of the Black Panther Party's use of the word "pig" to describe the police.

The quote by J. Edgar Hoover is from the final Church Committee report.

The purpose of the House Committee on Internal Security study of the Black Panther Party, as stated in the preface of its report: "to determine its origin, history, organization, character, objectives, and activities with particular reference to certain aspects set forth in the committee mandate." The mandate included investigations of groups seeking to "establish a totalitarian dictatorship within the United States, or to overthrow or assist in the overthrow of the form of government of the United States or any State thereof." For information about incidents of sabotage against the BPP newspaper, see *Black Panther*, August 8, 1970.

Chapter 3 of this book discusses the decline of the publication of the *Black Panther* newspaper. See the December 29, 1978, special issue of the *Black Panther* about the mass deaths of members of the People's Temple in Jonestown, Guyana. The People's Temple was founded by the Rev. Jim Jones, who died at Jonestown. The BPP had developed a close relationship with the People's Temple, whose community programs for poor people in San Francisco and Northern California were much like those of the party. Charles Garry, a longtime attorney for the BPP, was also the attorney for the People's Temple. The BPP believed that People's Temple members voluntarily moved to Guyana to flee racism and poverty in the United States, which the party considered a serious indictment of life in America. See also Michael Meirs, *Was Jonestown a CIA Experiment? A Review of the Evidence*, Studies in American Religion (Edwin Mellen Press, 1989).

The quote by Father Earl A. Neil is from the "The Role of the Church and the Survival Program," *Black Panther,* May 15, 1971.

The quote from Tanya Russell is from the July 15, 1993, interview.

The quote by Bobby Seale about hunger and poverty in America is from *Seize the Time.*

The quote from the *Wall Street Journal* is from Foner, *The Black Panthers Speak.*

The description of the FBI's sabotage of the BPP's Free Breakfast Program is discussed in the Church Committee report and in Charles E. Jones, "The Political Repression of the Black Panther Party 1966–1971: The Case of the Oakland Bay Area," *Journal of Black Studies* 18 (1988).

The quote by Assata Shakur is from *Assata: An Autobiography* (Lawrence Hill, 1987).

The quote by Elaine Brown about the BPP food giveaways is from *A Taste of Power.*

The information about the various BPP free health clinics is from the previously cited doctoral dissertation by Kit Kim Holder, "The History of the Black Panther Party 1966–1972." Jake Winters, a member of the Chicago BPP, and two Chicago policemen died during a shootout on November 13, 1969. See Kenneth O' Reilly's book *Racial Matters: The FBI's Secret File on Black America, 1960–1972* (Free Press, 1989).

For more information about the BPP's sickle cell anemia program, see David Hilliard and Lewis Cole, *This Side of Glory: The Autobiography of David Hilliard and the Story of the Black Panther Party* (Lawrence Hill, 2001) and the following articles in the *Black Panther*: "Black Genocide: Sickle Cell Anemia," April 10, 1971; "The People's Fight against Sickle Cell Anemia

Begins," May 22, 1971; and "BPP Trains Houstonians for Free Medical Testing Program," June 22, 1974.

The information about the Winston-Salem Free Ambulance Service is from "Winston-Salem Free Ambulance Service Opens," *Black Panther,* February 16, 1974. Joseph "Joe-Dell" Waddell was a member of the Winston-Salem, North Carolina, branch of the BPP. On June 12, 1972, he was pronounced dead of a heart attack at Central Prison in Raleigh, North Carolina. His fellow inmates believed that prison authorities gave Waddell drugs to induce heart failure. See also Mario Van Peebles, Ula Y. Taylor, and J. Tarika Lewis, *Panther: A Pictorial History of the Black Panthers and the Story behind the Film* (Newmarket Press, 1995); and *Black Panther*, February 16, 1974.

For more about the BPP's educational programs, see Newton, *Revolutionary Suicide*; G. Louis Heath, *Off the Pigs! The History and Literature of the Black Panther Party* (The Scarecrow Press, 1976); Holder, "The History of the Black Panther Party 1966–1972"; and *Black Panther*, March 27, 1971.

The Oakland Community Learning Center (OCLC) offered a variety of educational and recreational programs, including GED classes and martial arts classes. Various community groups in Oakland, such as the Black Veterans Association, met regularly at the OCLC. See *Black Panther,* January 29, 1977; and Brown, *A Taste of Power*. Former BPP member Carol Granison and I wrote the curriculum for language arts taught at the Oakland Community School (OCS). I was also a language arts instructor at OCS from 1976 to 1981. For more about OCS programs, see *Black Panther*, June 22, 1974, and April 2, 1977.

For more about the "Pocket Lawyer," see Newton, *Revolutionary Suicide.*

Articles from the August 8, 1970, and October 1–14, 1979, issues of the *Black Panther* discuss the BPP's prison work. According to Elaine Brown, writing in *A Taste of Power*, "The Black Panther Party provided a voice and a hope for thousands of Black inmates."

For more about Herbert Haines's analysis, see his *Black Radicals and the Civil Rights Mainstream, 1954–1970.*

Robert Staples, *The Urban Plantation: Racism and Colonialism in the Post Civil Rights Era* (Black Scholar Press, 1987).

Among some of the earlier autobiographies published by former

BPP members are *Revolutionary Suicide* by Huey P. Newton; *A Lonely Rage* by Bobby Seale; *A Taste of Power* by Elaine Brown; *This Side of Glory* by David Hilliard and Lewis Cole; *My Life with the Black Panther Party* by Akua Njeri (formerly Deborah Johnson); *Assata: An Autobiography* by Assata Shakur (formerly Joanne Chesimard); and *A Long Time Gone* by William Lee Brent. Some of the rap artists who performed material about the Black Panther Party are Public Enemy and the late Tupac Shakur. The 1995 film *Panther*—a fictional account of the BPP's early days—was based on a screenplay written by Melvin Van Peebles and directed by his son, Mario.

For discussions about the structure and decision-making process of the Black Panther Party, see Hilliard and Cole, *This Side of Glory* and Brown, *A Taste of Power*.

For more about the repression of the Black Panther Party, see the Church Committee report cited above; Jones, *The Black Panther Party [Reconsidered]*; and Ward Churchill and Jim Vander Wall, *Agents of Repression: The FBI's Secret Wars Against the Black Panther Party and the American Indian Movement* (South End Press, 1988).

The quote at the end of the chapter is from Huey Newton, "On the Defection of Eldridge Cleaver from the Black Panther Party and the Defection of the Black Panther Party from the Black Community," *Black Panther*, April 17, 1971.

Chapter 7

The title of Chapter 7, "The Party Was Irresistible," is taken from a July 15, 1993, interview with Melvin Dickson.

The role of the police in sparking the 1965 rebellion in Watts is discussed in Bennett, *Before the Mayflower: The Report of the National Advisory Commission on Civil Disorders* discusses the role of the police as a factor in the 1967 rebellions in Detroit and Newark, New Jersey.

The complete text of the October 1966 Ten-Point Platform and Program of the Black Panther Party for Self-Defense may be found on the website of It's About Time: Black Panther Party Legacy and Alumni, www.itsabouttimebpp.com/home/bpp_program_platform.html.

The information about the backgrounds of Huey P. Newton and Bobby Seale and the founding of the Black Panther Party comes primarily from Newton, *Revolutionary Suicide*, and Seale, *Seize the Time*.

The "greatest single threat" quote by J. Edgar Hoover and the statistics on the FBI COINTELPRO actions against the BPP come from the Church Committee report.

The quotes and statements by Melvin Dickson are from the previously cited July 15, 1993, interview.

For more about the BPP's socialist ideology, see Huey P. Newton's 1971 essay, "Intercommunalism," in *The Huey P. Newton Reader* (Seven Stories Press, 2002).

Quotes and statements by Fahim Minkah (formerly known as Fred Bell) are from a September 8, 1996, interview.

For more about the Dallas BPP chapter, see Skip Shockley, "The History of the Black Panther Party, Dallas and North Texas," www.itsabouttimebpp.com/Chapter_History/Dallas_Chapter_BPP_2.html.

Ernie McMillan says that while out of jail on bond awaiting the appeal of his sentence, his attorney told him that he had violated his bond agreement by leaving Texas in June 1969, for an out-of-state speaking engagement. McMillan subsequently fled from Dallas. Captured by police in Ohio in 1971, he was incarcerated in federal and Texas prisons until his release in 1975. See the "Ernest McMillan," Civil Rights Movement Archive, www.crmvet.org/vet/mcmille.htm.

In a September 7, 1996, interview, Charles Beasley said that to avoid prosecution he fled to Canada, where he was imprisoned for two years for attempting to hijack a plane to Cuba. In 1970 he was deported to the United States, where he served thirteen years in Texas and federal prisons. He was released in 1982.

Quotes and statements by Charles "Boko" Freeman are from a July 10, 1993, interview.

Quotes and statements by Ayanna Ade (formerly known as Gwen Johnson) are from a September 5, 1996, interview.

Quotes and statements by Tondalela Woolfolk are from a June 13, 1992, interview.

Epilogue

The quote at the beginning of the chapter is from Peniel Joseph, "Black Liberation without Apology: Reconceptualizing the Black Power Movement," *Black Scholar*, Fall/Winter 2001.

Quotes and statements by Joyce Grant are from the previously cited August 3, 1993, interview.

Quotes and statements by Jackie Pope are from the previously cited August 15, 1993, interview.

Quotes and statements by Lee Rose are from the previously cited August 1, 1993, interview.

Quotes and statements by Joe Hicks are from the previously cited July 8, 1993, interview.

Quotes and statements by Rev. C. Herbert Oliver are from the previously cited August 14, 1993, interview.

Quotes and statements by Zakiya Somburu are from the previously cited July 20, 1993, interview.

Quotes and statements by Mike Hamlin are from the previously cited April 27, 1997, interview.

Quotes and statements by Tanya Russell are from the previously cited July 15, 1993, interview.